T0143611

DEFENSIVE TACTICS
for Today's Law Enforcement

STEPHEN K. HAYES • JOE NIEHAUS

CRC Press
Taylor & Francis Group
Boca Raton London New York

CRC Press is an imprint of the
Taylor & Francis Group, an **informa** business

CRC Press
Taylor & Francis Group
6000 Broken Sound Parkway NW, Suite 300
Boca Raton, FL 33487-2742

© 2017 by Taylor & Francis Group, LLC
CRC Press is an imprint of Taylor & Francis Group, an Informa business

No claim to original U.S. Government works

Printed in Canada on acid-free paper
Version Date: 20160825

International Standard Book Number-13: 978-1-4987-7667-7 (Paperback)

Library of Congress Cataloging-in-Publication Data

Names: Hayes, Stephen K., author. | Niehaus, Joe, author.
Title: Defensive tactics for today's law enforcement / Stephen K. Hayes, Joe Niehaus.
Description: Boca Raton, FL : CRC Press, [2017] | Includes bibliographical references.
Identifiers: LCCN 2016022836| ISBN 9781498776677 (pbk.) | ISBN 1498776671 (pbk.) | ISBN 9781315410005 (web pdf) | ISBN 1315410001 (web pdf)
Subjects: LCSH: Self-defense for police. | Police--Violence against. | Law enforcement.
Classification: LCC HV8080.S34 H39 2017 | DDC 363.2/3--dc23
LC record available at https://lccn.loc.gov/2016022836

Visit the Taylor & Francis Web site at
http://www.taylorandfrancis.com

and the CRC Press Web site at
http://www.crcpress.com

This is dedicated to the men and women who are the Thin Blue Line.

Contents

Acknowledgments

The authors would like to thank the following for their assistance with the creation of this work.

Deb and Matt Barber
Pam Chambers
Nick Milner
Mat Niehaus
Dr. Robert Rice
Teresa Weimer
Pete Willis
Carolyn Spence.

Authors

Stephen K. Hayes has spent his entire adult life in the pursuit of perfection through the study of the Asian martial arts and spiritual traditions. He was born in Wilmington, Delaware, in 1949, and grew up in Dayton, Ohio. He has lived and traveled throughout North America, Japan, Europe, the Arctic, China, Tibet, Nepal, and India. A husband and father of two daughters, he is a writer, teacher, and ardent student of life. Stephen K. Hayes began his martial arts career in Ohio as a teenager in the 1960s. In 1985, he was elected to the prestigious Black Belt Hall of Fame for his years of pioneering work introducing the Japanese ninja martial arts to the Western world. In 1993, Grandmaster Masaaki Hatsumi of Chiba-ken, Japan, awarded him the extremely rare honor of ju-dan 10th degree Black Belt in the nine historical traditions of the Bujinkan Dojo martial arts.

Author of 20 books
Ambassador of Togakure Ryu Ninjutsu in the West
University adjunct professor
Apprentice in the home of the grandmaster of the ninja in Japan
Bodyguard for Nobel Peace Prize laureate the Dalai Lama of Tibet
Referred to by *Black Belt Magazine* as "one of the 10 most influential
    martial artists alive in the world today"

Joe Niehaus earned an AS in police science and a BS in criminal justice at the University of Cincinnati in Cincinnati, Ohio. He earned a master's degree in criminal justice: homeland security at Tiffin University in Tiffin, Ohio. He spent 36 years in the law enforcement field retiring as a lieutenant with the Kettering Police Department in Ohio, where he created the Defensive Tactics Program and developed one of the first Integrated Use of Force training programs in the United States. He has instructed police defensive tactics not only for Kettering but at regional and national police conferences and is a martial arts practitioner and personal student of Stephen K. Hayes and holds an instructor license in To Shin Do. He has published in magazines such as *Law and Order, Police Marksman, Police Magazine, The Law Enforcement Trainer, Close Quarter Combat, The Ohio Police Chief, Black Belt Magazine, Spirit of the Ninja,* and *Fighting Stars.* His articles also appeared in *The Best of Police*

Marksman Volume II. He has authored eight books including *Investigative Forensic Hypnosis* and *The Sixth Sense: Practical Tips for Everyday Safety.* He is currently an adjunct professor at Ashford University, San Diego, California; American Public University System (APUS), Charles Town, West Virginia; Tiffin University; and Sinclair Community College, Dayton, Ohio.

Introduction

I did not consider myself a fighter when I became a cadet with the Cincinnati Police Department in 1975. I had no prior training in fighting and what I knew I learned on the school grounds as a child. So when I entered the field of law enforcement, this topic quickly became something that I wanted to know more about.

My father was a police officer for 27 years. He went into the profession after serving in World War II. He was a carpenter by trade but work was hard to find in those days, so he noticed an ad for police officer with the City of Deer Park in Ohio and applied, landing the job. He jokingly described his training to me as, "I was sworn in, they gave me a badge, gun and a ticket book and said go get 'em." The idea of training even with the basic tools was very limited in his day, although he did go to the range and qualify several times a year.

So when I entered the police academy at Cincinnati, I quickly realized that I was not truly prepared for a real street fight where my life would be on the line. When we would go to the gym, the instructors were martial artists holding black belts in various arts. To say I was intimidated would be an understatement. When my name was called to face one of the more impressive black belts, I wanted to turn and run out of the room. But I knew as an officer that was not an option, so I stood there. As he moved in and took a swing at me, my head said I should stand my ground like the other cadets had done and meet him head to head—and lose as the others had done! But my body told me something else, it said move away and to the side—so I did.

I had successfully slipped the attack and had I been more aware I would have had the presence of mind to see the advantage I now held by facing his back and could easily apply a control hold or engage in a more aggressive manner. But after I had escaped, I was perhaps wondering what I should do next—and the look on the instructor's face as he looked back at me showed the shock and frustration at my move. It was not what he expected.

The session ended of course—and not well for me. The instructor wanted to make a point about my escape as there were a few snickers in the gym. I was left however with a lot of questions. To seek out answers, I also enrolled at a martial art studio in Covington, Kentucky. The art was Chito Ryu and was a fairly standard martial art, but it did not help me with my questions about moving around an opponent rather than meet them face on—strength to strength.

Later I became a Kettering Police officer in Kettering, Ohio and shortly after graduating from the Ohio State Patrol Police Academy, Columbus, Ohio, I enrolled at a Kung Fu studio to continue my martial arts training. This was similar to Chito Ryu and also did not provide the answer to my question from the training at Cincinnati and that is when things changed.

When I first met Stephen K. Hayes, I was barely into my police career of 36 years. At that time, I had just read a small paperback book that was a biography of various martial arts masters, and there was a chapter on this man who had brought Ninjutsu to America. So it was ironic what happened next.

I was working the dayshift when I was dispatched to a residence on a burglary alarm. I got there and was told by my dispatcher that backup was not available. So I checked the exterior of the residence and found it was secured. The dispatcher advised me that a family member with a key would be there to check the residence. As I was walking around the house, a man approached wearing a T-shirt that had a small ninja figure and the words "Ninjutsu the Art of Winning." I will add here that I thought the shirt was pretty cool and was going to ask him where he got it but thought that might not appear to be professional. The man looked familiar, but I did not put two and two together yet. For those of you who are officers, you know how annoying that is when you cannot put a name or reason with a face—we have no idea of course if they are friend or foe! We had a nice conversation and I learned that it was his parent's house, that they were away on vacation, and that he was close by.

Stephen K. Hayes and Dr. Masaaki Hatsumi wearing the "really cool" ninja shirt.

It was not until a dispatcher showed me the neighborhood paper later that week that there was an article on Stephen talking about him training in Kettering. That is when I realized I was talking to Stephen K. Hayes. The article in the paper gave some contact information, so I made the call and we met to train in of all places an old gravel pit near a cemetery.

From the first training session, I knew I had found something very applicable to the street and law enforcement. The art that Stephen taught was not the static arts I had experimented with before. It taught a whole new way of hitting using your whole body to carry the attack to your opponent and was completely revolutionary for the time. Being that I was not one of the biggest officers in the department; this certainly came in handy. Most importantly, when he demonstrated what he called the "wind" technique I knew I had found my answer. That is exactly what I did in response to that attack in the Cincinnati academy years before. You will find this later in Chapter 5.

Over the years Stephen would offer various techniques, but one thing he stressed was that we were not to take his word that the techniques were effective. He said that we should test them ourselves. Test them I did. I would be involved in various situations on the street and would apply some of the techniques that I had learned in class and was impressed that they worked. I would return to class and tell Stephen how I used this technique or that and under what circumstances.

Stephen and me instructing a class for ASLET (American Society of Law Enforcement Trainers) in Mobile, Alabama.

Over the years, Stephen's interest in law enforcement and applicable techniques increased. He would come to the department and climb into the cruiser with me for a shift on the street to see firsthand what an officer faces and how he could help improve on our ability to deal with it. Stephen even attended a national law enforcement training conference with me, and he even attended the RAD (Rape Aggression Defense) course that the Kettering Police Department would offer to the citizens. While at the conference Stephen was an avid student of the courses offered by other police trainers and when we would discuss them he would show how each of these could be enhanced using the body's natural tendencies.

Stephen, me, Larry Nadeau (instructor), Kathy Wright (instructor), and Rumiko Hayes after completing the RAD Instructor's Course (Rape Aggression Defense) at the Kettering Police Department in Ohio.

As time went on, I was tasked with setting up the Kettering Police Department's defensive tactics program. In order to do this, only approved defensive tactics programs were allowed by the chief. We brought in PPCT (Pressure Point Control Tactics) created by Bruce Siddle and what I found very interesting was that the approach to striking in that method verified what I had been learning from Stephen all those years.

While I developed the program at Kettering we introduced several other police defensive tactics programs and took what fit our program and refined our methods. What we found from developing this course was that the programs that followed the principle of keeping things simple and as natural as possible were received and implemented the best by our officers. This became an important part of what we sought to do with the program, keeping it as simple and close to what someone would tend to do naturally without extensive practice and training.

Even so, with all of this, something was missing. We developed one of the nation's first Integrated Use of Force training programs taking officers from verbal to deadly force in a training scenario. This greatly enhanced the abilities of the officers who underwent the training. As we offered this to other agencies, we quickly saw how better prepared Kettering's officers were because of the training program we had developed. But even so, something was missing.

The problem was that all of the programs we brought treated male and female officers the same. Large and small officers were expected to perform the same techniques no matter who they were going against. The level of force was the only change for officers depending on who they were facing.

I knew there was another way, a better way, to allow for our natural tendencies and physical differences. The art of Ninjutsu provided a method that allowed an officer four choices of applying the same technique depending on how they were reacting to the threat. Stephen and I presented this concept at a national police trainer's conference and received very positive responses. As a result, we present it here for you to add to you repertoire of abilities to keep you safer on the street and to enhance the tactics and training that we already have received or will receive in the future. But heed Stephen's words—do not take our word for it—test it for yourself and see if it makes you a more complete fighter.

Why Change Defensive Tactics Training

1

The best defense against a surprise attack is not to be "surprised."
—**Bruce Lee**
Bruce Lee's Fighting Method Basic Training, 1977

The subject of force and law enforcement has always been one that seeks constant improvement. Dealing with rapidly evolving situations, law enforcement personnel have had a variety of tools and skill training provided to them over the years. Some have been effective, and some have provided poor or mixed results. This quest for the most effective method of dealing with aggressive behavior is constant as our times and technology evolve.

The concept of police defensive tactics is a relatively new approach to the police and physical encounters. Basic police academy provided some training in such things as punches, kicks, dealing with choke-holds, and grabs. There was training in the handheld weapons such as a baton to deal with more aggressive subjects, but the idea of on-going training and improved training was not truly developed before the 1980s. New recruits were expected to already have had some kind of skill training in that area whether it came from the military or they earned it on the street. However, it was presumed that if you wanted to be a police officer, then you would have the ability to handle yourself in a physical encounter. However, the further police recruits moved from World War II, the Korean Wars, and the Vietnam War, the less likely a new recruit would have this skill set. There was also a shift in the hiring practices, and in an effort to become more professional, police departments sought more college graduates rather than people with military experience.

In the early 1990s, the Los Angeles Police Department set out to make a defensive tactics program that would encompass all of the skills that officers would need in facing the criminal element. They gathered martial arts experts in many different fields and brought them together to create this new and improved system. However, before they did that, they searched their use-of-force records to find the most common occurrences of force application for officers, as this would help determine what kind of techniques should be adapted.

The Los Angeles Police Department found the following situations:

1. The officer grabbed an individual by the arm, and the individual pulled away.
2. The suspect ran at the officer and attacked with arms and legs.
3. The suspect ran from the officer, which resulted in both officer and suspect going to the ground.
4. The suspect assumed a fighting stance but waited for the officer to approach.
5. The suspect was about to be handcuffed.

This resulted in the development of a program that included not only standard defensive tactics in punches and kicks but also ground fighting because that was often lacking in basic training programs for law enforcement. It is interesting to note that those same situations are prevalent today in suspect-police encounters.

The 1980s and 1990s saw the development of many effective defensive tactics programs that were based on practical street applications and experiences. Some of the major development programs were ones like Bruce Siddle's Pressure Point Control Tactics, which were adopted by many departments as basic academy defensive tactics training. Modern Warrior in New York created many realistic training opportunities by bringing more realism to the training and developing ground fighting and weapons training. Tony Blauer introduced his SPEAR technique to deal with the sudden assault situations that officers may face. FORCE created a, by the numbers, method of dealing with active aggression during arrest or violent encounter situations. Many other innovative programs were developed as well during this time. It seemed that the field was rich in the development of effective training for officers to deal with active aggressive suspects. Even so, with all of this development and skills, there were times when officers found themselves on the losing end and their skills failing them. The training and techniques were sound, so where was the weak link?

Law enforcement personnel did not always have to rely on just their hands to take on aggressive suspects. Throughout the years, different tools have been provided to them, which the public supported. The most common tool, of course, was the baton, which has evolved over the years from a wooden stick to the martial-arts-inspired PR-24 to the now metal collapsible baton. Once items such as saps and sap gloves were permitted, but these have been banned by most departments today. Even the flashlight was used as an impact weapon if the situation called for it. Many officers carried three and four D-cell flashlights that provided the required light at night and could be used as an impact weapon, but now that tool has been replaced by the smaller and more powerful tactical flashlight. The creation of mace was thought to be the new "self defense in a can" tool, but its effectiveness was very limited, as officers and suspects alike were usually sprayed and felt its effects.

Today, two options seem to be the preferred methods of many departments: the OC spray or pepper spray, which has mixed reviews from different sources and agencies, and the taser, which also has its supporters and opponents. As we look at such things as OC spray and the taser, officers are afforded the ability to diffuse a violent confrontation with these aids. However, these tools are not 100% effective, as many cases will attest. Because of that, officers must be ready and prepared to go to alternative force options to deal with the aggressive behavior. Officers still are acutely aware of the need for physical techniques that will enable them to go hands on with a suspect, and with that, there is a greater potential of injury not only to the suspect but also to the officer.

An interesting experiment conducted by Modern Warrior in New York revolved around the effectiveness of OC spray. They had volunteers who agreed to be sprayed with OC spray directly in the face. After the OC spray was sprayed on the face, the volunteers were given the task of walking the length of a pool, grabbing a knife placed on a table, and stabbing a target. In theory, OC spray should have made that very difficult for the volunteers to accomplish; however, during the test, they found that all of the participants were able to accomplish the mission, which put into doubt the ability of OC to be as effective as advertized, when the person has a goal or mission to accomplish.

While the taser has been the most effective "self-defense in a can" system to date, even this has some weakness. If both of the barbs from the taser do not encounter the subject's body or if the subject is wearing heavy clothing, the contact between the two barbs may not occur. Information has also been found that some inmates in prison practice twirling their shirt to catch the barbs, so that when they get out of prison and encounter this tool, they can counteract it. No tool is ever foolproof, and that is why officers need to be as complete as they possibly can be, when it comes to force options.

Officers receive empty-hand techniques training while going through their academy, and those skills are often enhanced with in-service training or even supplemented with training on their own. For a time, the use of force continuums helped to direct an officer's use of force when dealing with a rapidly evolving situation and authorized him or her to follow the plus one rule of being able to use one level of force above the resistive behavior. This type of training helped provide an understanding for the public and officers alike. Although the force continuum allowed for differences in officer's size and other such factors, it did not take into account an officer's emotional state at the time of attack.

Force continuum
Deadly force
Impact weapons
OC spray and taser
Hands-on techniques
Verbal commands
Officer's presence

The emotional state of an officer can have a major effect on whether or not the training that he or she had received and the techniques that he or she had learned will be effective. For example, an officer who may be like the Biblical David, who had to face Goliath, would find it unnerving perhaps to confront the huge Goliath in a head-to-head physical altercation. Following the force continuum, the officers should be able to go one level up and utilize some of the tools that have been provided to assist them, such as the taser, baton, and OC spray. However, what happens when there is not enough time to respond with one of the tools that an officer has readily available or the tool is ineffective when deployed, and as a result, the officer must rely on his or her hands-on techniques and skills? Will those skills be able to overcome the advantage of the aggressor? If the officer does move beyond that force level to a higher one, will it appear to the public that the officer is now using excessive force? The video camera that views an officer's actions will only see the action, not what the officer is experiencing, and this is an area that is left unexplored.

The issue of panic can cause multiple problems in a physical encounter. When someone is faced with a situation that his or her brain cannot analyze and cannot provide a suitable solution to, the brain freezes and so does the officer. A simple example is when you find yourself out somewhere, say at a shopping mall, and you come across someone you know. Their face is very familiar and you know him or her, but still, you cannot remember his or her name. The harder you try to remember the name, the less you are able to remember. This is a form of panic. Now, after the person leaves and the situation returns to normal, suddenly you can remember their name. This is how the brain works when we are panicked. Under great stress, solutions are not found because the conscious mind is overwhelmed with the situation. When this happens in a physical encounter, it can have devastating results.

Most police defensive tactics training programs treat officers in a "cookie-cutter" fashion in that one technique fits all, no matter the size or stature of the officer. The problem develops when an officer is required to execute a technique that his or her body is telling him or her to abandon. For example, imagine that you are faced with an opponent who is much larger than you are. If this subject charges you, do you truly want to meet him head on? Isn't there a moment where the natural thing to do is to retreat away from the charge? This is why some techniques, while valid and effective, fail in the execution. The body goes in one direction and the mind tries to steer it in another, which results is poor application of the technique.

The secret is to have the mind and the body on the same page, and then, the application of the technique will be more effective, and there will be a greater chance of stopping the aggressive behavior without injury. However, when you are David and facing Goliath, getting both the body and mind in sync can be a problem. In addition, the time needed to respond could be under seconds, leaving little time to process the attack and form an effective defense. Remember that the attacking suspect has the initial advantage, because he knows when he is going to launch his attack, and the officer must process this and then form a response, all of which takes time.

Basic police training in defensive tactics teaches the principle of the reactionary gap. This creates time on the side of an officer to notice an attack and form a response to the attack, allowing the officer to use distance to give him time. The closer an officer is to a suspect, the less time he will have to react to an attack. Therefore, good tactics teach that the officer needs a good distance, and the further the distance, the more time an officer will have to perceive the threat and respond to it. The recommended distance is about six feet. Although this sounds good in training, in reality, this distance is usually much closer on the street. Just imagine if all police officers stood six feet away from people they were dealing with. How friendly would that department seem, and would the community feel that they are truly fulfilling their needs? The whole concept of community-oriented policing is for officers to become more involved in the community, and this is not truly possible with a six feet standoff zone. Therefore, while this may be tactically sound, it is not going to be possible for an officer on the street because of the assignment and mission that he or she delivers to the public. While the six feet standoff area may be impractical, the officer should make use of what distance he can, to allow him to formulate a response to the attack—even a few steps will aid in dealing with a rapid attack.

Another basic tactic taught to officers is relative positioning. The concept comes from the work of James Morrell and one of his students, John Desmedt. Morrell designed the principle called the Three Levels of Avoidance, which gave a numbering system to guide officers on dealing with a subject and where backup officers could take better tactical positions. In this system, the position directly in front of a subject was named level three, as this is where the officer is open to all of the physical weapons that a person may possess. The position standing next to the subject on either side was level two, which is a good one for an escort or control position, and the position directly behind a subject was called level one, which presented few weapons from the subject but gave the officer the advantage of gaining control (Figure 1.1).

Relative positioning

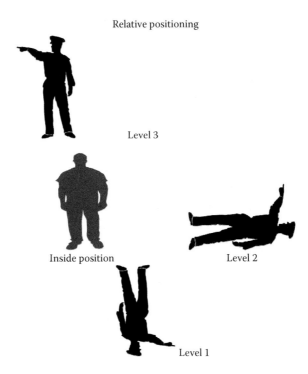

Level 3

Inside position   Level 2

Level 1

Figure 1.1 This chart demonstrates the three positions in the concept of relative positioning. Notice that the officer stays away from the inside position on the suspect to avoid being directly in front of the primary weapons of the suspect. (Courtesy of pixabay.com.)

Desmedt changed this a little by calling the position directly in front of a subject as the inside position. Then, he adjusted the positions around a subject to being slightly off center but still in front as being level 1; level 2 was the same as Morrell's, and this was from either side, but Desmedt added a level 2 and a half, which is where the officer is slightly offset but at the rear of a subject. Level 3 as per Desmedt was where the officer faced the back of the subject.

The ideal position for an officer for talking to someone on the street is to stand slightly off center of a subject, in a 45-degree angle. This off-set stance allows the officer to keep his primary weapon away from a suspect and to have his body bladed in the case of an attack. This gives an officer a bit of an edge in dealing with a subject who suddenly turns aggressive. This is not a new concept, as martial arts have utilized such thinking for ages, but it again does not solve the total problem of a sudden attack from a suspect. If David is facing Goliath, there will be the mind-body connection that needs to be in total agreement for tactics and techniques to work effectively.

However, officers often find themselves in situations where they may not be in the ideal position. Officers go into residences, businesses, alleys, and more, finding that there may not be enough room to establish the safe distance and bladed stance. In addition, the officer's natural tendencies and the situation can deteriorate quickly.

Phil Messina of Modern Warrior brought to the light the concept of "time-framing" during a fight. The idea is that during a confrontation, there are blocks of time on both sides of the fight. The problem for the officer is that he is usually lagging behind the suspect's time frame in the initial portion of the fight. This is because the suspect has already shifted into the fighting frame of mind, planned the attack, and initiated it. On the other hand, the officer has to shift from his current thoughts to those of defense—this means that he has lost valuable time—he is reacting to an action that has already occurred. The only way to make up time frames is to utilize distance and apply sound tactics.

So, how can we begin to increase reaction time for officers? One way for officers to help them detect a potential attack is to use their skills as observers and to pay attention to the physical cues that are given off from a person just before initiating an attack (Figure 1.2). By observing a person's body language, an officer can begin to prepare himself mentally and start to develop a plan of attack or defense should the attack occur (Figure 1.3).

Figure 1.2 Sometimes, it is easy to observe and articulate the actions of others. They telegraph their intentions by verbal and physical actions. (Courtesy of pixabay.com.)

Figure 1.3 Look at the man in this photograph. What can you tell about the indications that he is showing you? (Courtesy of pixabay.com.)

The following are some of the physical signs someone may give before launching an attack. Keep in mind that like most gestures, these possibly will come in clusters or they may not. This list, by no means, covers all of the physical cues, but it is provided here to give the reader an idea of what some of these gestures are.

- Conspicuously ignoring the officer's verbal commands
- Exaggerated movements—swinging arms, waving arms, etc.
- Dressing down—taking off a hat, watch, or other garment
- Facial color change
- Change from uncooperative subject to suddenly cooperative subject
- Clenching fists
- Ceasing all movement
- Fighting stance
- Shift in their shoulder
- Target glance—looking where they want to attack
- Depersonalizing the officer
- Increased body movement
- Unusual sounds—grunting and growling
- Lowering their center of gravity
- Lack of verbalization

- Distraction technique—trying to split the officer's attention
- Facial wipe
- "Million mile" stare—looking as if they do not see anyone

Officers should watch for these cues to come in clusters—which are multiple gestures in a short period of time. If this is observed, it gives time to the officer to prepare a response and he should increase his or her awareness. Even so, with the reactionary gap, the tactical stance, and observation skills, an officer may still have to prepare for an assault from an opponent that he may not want to go head to head with.

There is the issue of confidence. In order to implement an offensive tactic against a larger and perhaps faster and better-trained opponent, an officer will need confidence in his abilities to perform the technique properly. Here is one of the areas where police training is very important. Officers actually train more with their firearm than they do with physical confrontation techniques, even though the latter will be more likely used during the course of their career. The more confidence an officer has in his abilities, the more likely he will be able to execute the technique correctly and effectively. As the old saying goes, practice makes perfect—practice also never hurts performance.

However, if an officer has confidence, then the David-and-Goliath situation will or should be mitigated by the officer's training and techniques. It is this confidence that also keeps the officer's mind and body together and enable him to perform the techniques. But if there is that momentary hesitation, then an officer may need another edge to allow him to go with what his body wants him to do and his mind even if they are going in different directions.

There are several things that can aid an officer in boosting confidence. The first is practice and training in the hands-on techniques that he has learned. One of the reasons martial artists practice a technique over and over is to drill it into the brain and body. If this training is not burned into both, then in a time of crisis, the body and mind will revert usually to the first thing they had learned, and so, the officer may find himself fighting like he did in grade school. The military also drills techniques into soldiers, because under the extreme stress of battle, there is no time to think—the body and mind must be on the same page and respond based on training. Therefore, an officer who takes the time and effort to train on a regular basis will gain confidence in those skills and will not hesitate when faced with a highly stressful situation. The reality though is with shift hours, court time, family demands and more an officer may find that to be consistent in their training will be difficult, which is all the more reason to take advantage of every edge they can gain.

The next issue that can affect confidence is physical fitness. Someone who takes care of himself, maintains a healthy body weight, has aerobic capacity, and practice strength training has a much better chance in a violent encounter than someone who does not. When we are in good physical shape, we tend to respond quicker and last longer, when it comes to physical struggles. Therefore, it only adds to a person's confidence if he has maintained his fitness level. This does not mean that you have to be on the level of a professional athlete, but consistent physical training in both aerobics and strength trainings added to training with the skills techniques taught to officers will increase their confidence in being able to handle an aggressive subject on the street.

However, even officers who have done all of these things have found themselves to be poorly executing their techniques when faced with a Goliath and they have only a second or two to respond to the attack. Why would this happen? This comes back again to the mind-body issue. We are all humans and have some basic instincts. When faced with a situation where our mind tells us to do one thing but our body tells us to go in another direction, there can be conflict, which results in poor execution of the technique. It can also be as simple as that even with all of this, the attacker is so much larger or faster than the officer is that the technique is not applicable in an effective manner.

So, how does an officer overcome this and develop into a more skilled adversary, so that his or her training and skills can be applied in the most effective manner? The secret may rest with a centuries-old martial art and with listening to our natural fight and flight instincts.

Foundation of Defensive Tactics Training

2

The art of mobility ____ is the essence of fighting.
If you're slow on your feet, ____ you'll be late in hitting.
A skilled fighter can shift ____ to evade most blows.
His body is "light as a feather," ____ when he fights all foes.
He moves like a stallion ____ galloping with grace
Instead of a kangaroo ____ leaping high in space.

—Bruce Lee
Bruce Lee's Fighting Manual Basic Training, 1977

When it has come to the development of police defensive tactics, especially the hands-on tactics, the law enforcement community has often looked to the martial arts for answers. One of the primary reasons for this is that the methods of hand-to-hand combat have been documented, tested, and applied in the field in martial arts for centuries. There is a reason and purpose to each technique—the key, however, is to know what that purpose of the technique is and if it still applies in the world today.

For example, some of the punching techniques found in an art such as Okinawan Karate are very strong, powerful punches, but the goal of the attack is what needs to be looked at. The attack was designed to fight Samurai warriors, who were armored with bamboo and wielded a deadly weapon with great skill. The warriors of Okinawa had to be able to develop an attack that would penetrate that armor and give them the edge to survive the fight. However, the technique when applied today as it was taught would be awkward and avoidable by today's fighter, who is trained to be more mobile and agile, as we see in some of these mixed martial arts fights.

So, law enforcement needs to be careful when adopting martial arts techniques. While tested and developed over many years, the application needs to be appropriate in today's litigious society. The wrong technique adopted and added to a general order and then applied on the street can get the officer and department into some legal entanglements, which could be avoided with research.

When the Los Angeles Police Department developed their defensive tactics program in the 1990s, they gathered many martial artists from across the spectrum to bring their art and look at the common problems that officers face. The program they developed pulled from all of their arts to help form a program that would apply these age-old techniques to the modern world. One art, however, was missing from the mix.

In the early 1980s, an art was introduced to the United States that took the nation by storm. This art was known as Ninjutsu. It was a 900-year-old survival art that had been shrouded in mystery for centuries to protect those who practiced it. Misinformation about the art was distributed widely as a way to also conceal the true facts and techniques that the art held. Popular media, television, movies, and books quickly jumped on the bandwagon and helped perpetuate the myth that had surrounded these warriors of Japan. There were some who did seek out the truth behind their training and methods, and today, they understand better what the truth is. Although the veil had been lifted and the art grew in popularity, some misperceptions still persist today.

One of the reasons it grew so quickly was that it incorporated more than just punches, kicks, and takedowns. The art was a total street-survival system that included ground fighting, evasion, and other skills that were not found in the majority of martial arts at the time. It introduced the concept of using the total body mass when delivering punches and kicks, which was also different from the more static forms of traditional martial arts of the day. What was interesting to note is that some private police defensive tactics programs sought out scientific methods of delivering the most effective strikes and kicks, and they found that using total body mass—having the body behind each offensive movement—increased the amount of impact of that movement. This research just verified what had been in practice for centuries and presented in the art of Ninjutsu.

However, another aspect of the art of Ninjutsu was the concept of having multiple responses to an attack, based on the mind-body experience at the time. This concept made the techniques of total body even more effective, because practitioners found that they were more adept at dealing with an opponent if they could now consider their natural body movements and add to them the techniques developed over centuries of battle.

This fits in very well with the needs of law enforcement officers in our society. Each officer, although he or she wears a uniform, is still a person—the same person he or she was before he or she put on the uniform. Because of that, each one has his or her own fears, doubts, skills, and abilities—no two persons are exactly alike. Each of us also has experiences from life that are different and carry forward to how we interact with others, especially with those who are being aggressive toward us. For example, an officer who had served in the military and saw combat is more comfortable with an aggressive situation than an officer who grew up and was never involved in a hand-to-hand fight. The experienced serviceman will have had past experience to allow him to deal with the situation in a more confident manner than the other officer, simply because experience does help. Although both officers would have received the same training in the academy and in-service training, the one more comfortable or confident in the encounter will handle it more efficiently.

Ninjutsu presented a view that showed that we have basically four responses to an attack. By providing these options, officers can adapt the technique to the situation that they are facing and apply the skills and abilities that they have to their natural tendencies to increase their chance for success and survival.

Pre-Emptive Attack

The one that most police agencies rely on and most defensive tactics programs present would be to meet the attack as soon as it is detected or what might be called a pre-emptive response. Here, an officer, for example, could see someone clench and unclench his or her fists and start to move about in an agitated state. The officer makes a decision to intervene and so moves quickly to the subject to engage him or her. This action would be in line with what the majority of techniques and training present to officers. There is a reason behind this as well, because the officer will be in the position to dictate how the encounter will go as he or she is basically making the first move and has planned out the response to the cues given from the suspect.

Strategic Attack

Contrast that with an officer who now finds that he or she is squaring off with a suspect who is much larger than he or she is   much like the David and Goliath example in Chapter 1. Here, the officer will want to add more time on his or her side to help him or her deflect the incoming attack and perhaps prepare his or her response. This could be an example of a James Bond-type character who is faced with some incredible opponents but uses time and space to help defeat them. In a case like this, the officer may retreat backward at an angle to draw the aggressor out more, and then, when the attack has been avoided, the officer can move in with his or her counterattack and deal with the suspect. In both of these examples, the end result is that the officer stops the aggressive behavior, but as we see in both of them, the approach is different and the officer's reaction to the attack is different. Neither one is better than the other, it is just which one fits more in line with what the officer is observing and how appropriate he or she feels he or she can deal with the attack. We could think of the second response as a tactical response, because the officer is becoming more of a tactician in observing the attack and looking for a weakness to exploit.

Evasive Attack

Another option open for an officer when facing an incoming attack could be called evasive. Here, the officer's first move is to get out of the way of the attack completely. A method to do this is to move around the suspect, being where the suspect does not expect the officer to move. It becomes as if the suspect is fighting the wind; as the suspect moves, the officer moves from side to side but always alongside the suspect, so that suspect's attack moves by as the officer moves away. This also will give the officer an ability to strike back and gain control of a subject, because by moving alongside the attack, it will expose more vulnerable targets on the suspect for the officer to exploit. Think of it this way. If you were faced with a friend who had become agitated with you but you did not want to fight him or her, merely control him or her, so that he or she did not hurt you and you did not hurt him or her—this kind of movement would permit you to get in a position where you could gain a control hold on him or her and yet no injury would occur to either party. Similar to the tactical response yet tweaked to give an officer another option—again though, the techniques applied by the officer will be the same no matter which option they chose, that remains constant. What changes is their initial movement, which provides the officer the opportunity to respond to the attack.

Ground-Holding Attack

The fourth response from an officer could be called a ground-holding attack. Here, the officer believes that he or she is in full control, he or she sees the threat coming, knows that he or she can easily deal with it, and responds to it followed by his or her technique. You might think of it as a situation where you are faced with an opponent on whom you have the advantage, perhaps the reverse of the David and Goliath situation of the example found in the tactical response. Imagine yourself facing a child. You would not be intimidated by his or her attack and could easily brush it aside, but at the same time, you would apply enough force to control the child and no more. This kind of response puts the officer in the controlling situation, where he or she can minimize force and reduce the risk of an excessive force complaint.

Each of these options is natural human responses to the same attack, but each one responds in a different manner, permitting the officer to be aware of the danger, how he or she initially views the attack, and then moves his or her body to a position that will permit him or her to utilize his or her training in an effective manner to deal with the threat. The ideal situation would be for an officer to be able to move from option to option fluidly, depending on the situation, without having to think about his or her initial response but just reacting to the attack. Given that an officer may have mere seconds to respond by going with his or her natural tendencies, the ability to match the mind-body response with that of the attack is much higher. The officer can better utilize his or her training and techniques that he or she has developed over the course of his or her career.

What follows will be a more detailed look at each of these responses and how it would look if applied. Again, the important thing to note is that the techniques and training that an officer has or that a department has adopted can easily fit into this, as we are looking at an officer's initial response to an aggressive attack.

However, before we go there, there are two building blocks that officers should have in place to ensure that they get the most out of their training and increase their effectiveness in a confrontation.

Mental Conditioning

While running radar, you notice a brown sedan drift between lanes and suddenly jerk back. Knowing this type of erratic driving to be a sign that the driver is under the influence of alcohol or drugs, you pull out and begin to follow. The car is occupied by a male driver and a female passenger, both of whom appear to be oblivious to the traffic hazard that they are becoming. After turning on your overhead lights without getting a response, you hit the siren.

The driver immediately applies the breaks and screeches to a halt on the side of the road. After notifying the dispatcher, you begin your approach on the driver's side. Suddenly, your attention is drawn to the female passenger who is holding a small caliber firearm to the driver's neck.

"Officer," she screams. "If you don't leave, I'm going to kill him. He's my no good ex-husband and I've had enough!" What would you do?

This very scenario was used as part of a lateral review process to hire an officer candidate. Alarmingly, many of the officers' responses showed lack of thought or insight into a situation like this, even though most of them had several years experience on the street.

Mental preparation has always been first among the skills needed for survival. In the situation mentioned earlier, what questions would go through your mind? Should I draw my gun first? Should I go for cover, and if so, where? Can I use deadly force, and if so, when would it be appropriate? Should I call for assistance, and if so, where would I direct them?

Questions such as these are the mental games needed to stimulate our thoughts, so that when faced with an unfamiliar situation, our brains will have some kind of basis for making a decision.

At a national police training conference, Sam Barber, one of the instructors, repeated a quote that carries a lot of weight. He said, "The body can't go where the mind hasn't been." This is very true in many areas but particularly in law enforcement. That is why training and experience are so important for survival during a violent confrontation. Fortunately, there are ways to prepare oneself for these encounters.

While on patrol, begin to play "what if" games with yourself. As you pull into a parking lot and approach a closed business, ask yourself, what would you do if someone suddenly came out carrying a firearm? Where would you stop your patrol vehicle? What would you use for cover? What escape route would you use in case you are overwhelmed with firepower? There are no limits to this. Many academies include this thought in their training of new recruits, so that the officer has thought a situation like this through.

The way the brain works is that when we are under stress, the mind searches for a similar situation or experience, so that we can understand how to react to the situation. This is why some people freeze in dangerous situations or they react very strangely, and we sometimes wonder why they did that. The answer is that the brain had no viable situation to link to this and panic set in, so we began to respond in our basic instincts.

The mental game also plays out in a defensive tactics situation. This is one of the reasons that martial artist practice katas over and over again, so that the brain understands that this is a proper response to this type of an attack. An officer must be prepared for any kind of situation, and yet, many will not face some situations until they find themselves in it. What can they do?

Just like the planning on patrol, the officer can play "what if" games with themselves. After being on a call, begin to ask yourself, what if that person had moved toward me in an aggressive manner, how would I have reacted? Where were my feet positioned? Could I have moved out of the way? Could I have deflected an assault? Another possibility is to utilize visualization exercises and mentally play out entire scenarios in your mind's eye. By planning out in your mind first, the brain will have a foundation to work from when confronted by the real situation.

An example of the importance of this can be found in a defensive tactics training in-service class taught to the Kettering Police Department in Ohio. A veteran officer of five years reviewed the defensive tactics techniques authorized by the department and was then confronted with a training scenario and an aggressive subject. Because the subject's size intimidated the officer, he did not utilize any of his techniques but ran and jumped on the attacking trainer. The result was not what the training looked for. It did show, however, that even though the officer had been shown the techniques, he was not able to apply them to a realistic situation because the brain froze.

Mental training is vital, as Mr. Barber said, "the body can't go where the brain hasn't been."

Mental training is the first step in defensive tactics!

Physical Fitness

Physical fitness is another form of training that is also necessary for officers and is the one that is as important as all other forms. This cannot be stressed enough that an officer must maintain a level of fitness in order to survive a fight situation. In boxing matches, the rounds are short three-minute rounds, and at the end of each round, the boxers need a breather because they have expended themselves. In a fight on the street, there are no breaks, and an officer may have to fight off one or more attackers for a much longer time. Fitness is extremely important. In his book, *Box Like the Pros*, boxing champion and legend Smokin' Joe Frazier stressed the need to do "road work." No matter what the skill level a boxer may have, he or she must have endurance and leg strength to be able to handle the rigors of the boxing ring. His words are very true for the officers who find themselves involved in a fight; calling for backup is wise, but how long will you be able to deal with the aggressor until that backup arrives?

There are many resources on the subject of fitness, so it will not be delved in detail here. Officers should maintain a regular fitness program, if for nothing else, than to improve their health. Most police agencies do not require a fitness program, and so, once an officer leaves the academy, there are no requirements for them to maintain their fitness level. When you combine that with shift work, court, family obligations and perhaps even higher education classes a fitness regimen can be quickly brushed aside and as time goes on so too does an officer's ability to hold their own in a fight.

Of course, if you have been idle for some time, it is wise to seek out your physician to make sure that there are no issues that you need to be concerned with before starting a fitness program. One test that is often used by police agencies to test recruits and to check on officers' fitness is the mile and a half run. This run is long enough so that you must have some endurance but you must also be fast enough to meet time limits. This is a good judge for your aerobic fitness level.

It is advisable to have a regular aerobic fitness program to keep your endurance levels high. Today, we have many options available from popular at-home programs, local gyms, crossfit style training, and many, many more. The important thing is to do as World Champion Joe Frazier said, "you have to get the road work in."

Aerobics alone will not be enough. There are many who have great aerobic capability and yet no upper body strength. As an officer, aerobic ability may be great, as you can catch the suspect who is running away from you, but you will also need strength to deal with the suspect after you have caught him or her. Again, there are many effective programs available on strength training, from home gyms to professional ones. The important thing, like aerobics, is to get some form of strength training and maintain a regular routine. In the long term, there are many benefits of both these types of training that will outlast a career in law enforcement.

Preparation

Before we move on to the next section, there are a few items to keep in mind. The first is that these techniques are broken down into tiny segments of a physical confrontation. Think of them as snapshots at different times in a fight. They are not meant to be static in that once you complete the technique, you stop moving. On the contrary, you must move and continue to move until the fight has been won. You may find that a certain technique does not work right away—do not force the issue. If it does not work, immediately move to something else. You may ask, why? Because you do not have time to continue on something that is not working! For example, if you take the game of football and you find that every time you run the ball, the defensive line stops you. If you continue to run the ball, then you will lose the game. The same is true in a fight; if a technique is not working, then change to something else. There is no exact science in any fight, and each opponent offers a different set of problems.

Another thing to know before moving forward is how to make a fist. This may sound like common sense, but there is a way to make it, so that the fist is solid and you reduce the risk of injury to yourself. To do this, take your hand and extend the fingers. Now, curl your fingers toward your palm very tightly. When they have completely closed, there should be no gaps and the fist should feel very solid. The thumb should squeeze into the bottom of the first two fingers. This is the proper way to create a fist. Now you can just close your fingers and make a fist, but the curling of the fingers makes this a more solid surface and offers support to your fingers (Figures 2.1 and 2.2).

When you punch with your fist, the ideal striking surface is the first two knuckles. These are the biggest fingers on the hand and offer the largest surface of the hand to impact the intended target. If you find that you hit with the smaller fingers on the hand, you will run the risk of injury to the hand. Breaking the smaller bones is often called a boxer's break, and it can incapacitate that hand if you land in the wrong place.

The palm heel strike is another one you will want to know. This is where your striking surface is the heel of your palm. As you extend your arm toward

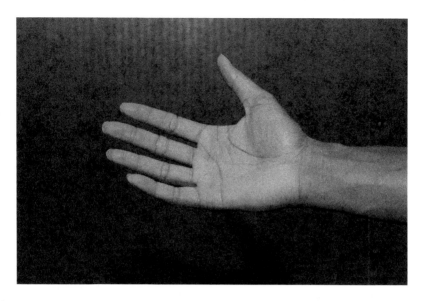

Figure 2.1 Start with the fingers extended and then begin to curl the fingers inward at each joint.

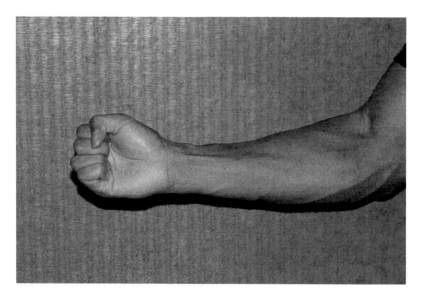

Figure 2.2 The hand and fingers should be solid, with no give, and the thumb should rest across the first two knuckles.

the target, to strike with the palm, turn your thumb up like you are pointing to the sky with it and curl your fingers from the first joint to the third. This will provide you with a very strong striking surface, as you are using the large bones in the body (Figures 2.3 and 2.4).

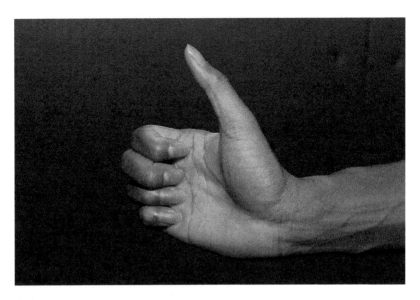

Figure 2.3 The palm heel strike should have the fingers curled back, with the thumb pointing upward. This will align the palm with the bone in the forearm for a strong, powerful strike.

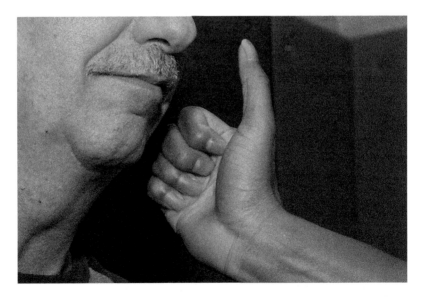

Figure 2.4 The palm heel strike is designed to go against large, strong targets like a jaw—it basically places the large bones of one against the strong bone surface of another.

The elbow strike is just that: using your elbow to deliver a blow. This can be delivered in any direction, and you are using the large part of your arm, including the elbow, to hit your target (Figures 2.5 and 2.6).

The reason you want to know these three strikes is that each one provides you with an advantage, depending on your target. For example, if you hit someone in the face with your fist, you are using the small bones in your hand to go against the large bones in your opponent's skull. There is a greater chance that your small bones will not fare well. However, if you use the palm heel strike in that instance, it will be your large bones going against their large bones and you have a better chance of staying in the fight.

Figure 2.5 The elbow strike is a very powerful but a close-in weapon. Keep in mind that your opposite hand should provide a defensive posture.

Figure 2.6 The elbow strike can be delivered in any direction but primarily from the side and an upward and downward direction.

When it comes to kicking, the simple rule is to kick with the ball of your foot, not your toes. In order to do this, you curl your foot backward, and you deliver the kick. When you do this, it keeps the small bones of your toes out of the way, while the larger striking surface of your foot does the damage. Just think about if you had to kick a door. What part of your foot do you want to impact on that door? That is exactly how you want to deliver a kick then (Figure 2.7).

Now, let's take a look at how we can enhance those defensive tactics techniques and our mind and body working as one.

Figure 2.7 When it comes to the kick, think of it as how you would kick a door. Keep your toes back and use the ball of your foot.

The Pre-Emptive Response

3

Do not be tense, just be ready, not thinking but not dreaming, not being set but being flexible. It is being "wholly" and quietly alive, aware and alert, ready for whatever may come.
—Bruce Lee
Bruce Lee Jeet Kune Do, 1997

You win battles by knowing the enemy's timing, and using a timing which the enemy does not expect
—Miyamoto Musashi
A Book of Five Rings, 1645

When it comes to defensive tactics, it is always a good idea to start with what is familiar and then build upon that. Most police training in the area of hands-on techniques requires that the officer move toward the attack and to overcome it. Indeed, when you read most police agencies' Use of Force General Orders, it mentions to use the force necessary to stop the aggression. So, by that indication, the officer needs to move to the aggression and resolve it. This is also much of what the public expects from law enforcement officers. They are expected to use their observation skills to understand the threat that they are facing and then to deal with it in the most efficient way. They are presumed to use just the force necessary to stop the attack facing the officer or a citizen if the officer is intervening.

The pre-emptive response to an attack is meant to intercept the attack. Just as the name implies, the officer is pre-emptive in dealing with the attack. Observation and understanding play a key role in directing the actions of the officers, as they must perceive the threat, understand that it is a threat, and then launch a response before the attack can be carried out successfully. So, the officer observes the indications that an attack is about to happen, say, for example, the fists clenching and unclenching, target glance, and perhaps a test aggressive step toward the officer; all are the indicators that the person before the officer is going to use violence, and yet, an attack has not yet been launched. The officer must keep a keen eye out for the movement that does signal the initiation of an attack, and then, the officer responds by going on the offensive. This is a high-energy type of response to an attack, because the officer is observant and understands the body gestures and mannerisms of the person in front of him. The response then is to take the fight to the suspect. This is what many police defensive tactics techniques are designed for.

The officer, of course, may not always be able to detect the attack before it is launched, but the response of taking the fight to the suspect is the same. The footwork applies the same, and the body moves forward into the attack as a response.

A breath response to help illustrate the movement and flow of the response is to say the word "hey" and notice the body's natural tendency. As you say "hey," you tend to be leaning forward, on the balls of your feet, moving toward who or what you are talking to. This verbal response helps embody the response of the body in this frame of mind. It could also be a verbal response given by the officer, as he initiates his response. Those who are bystanders, watching what is going on, will hear the officer's words of intervention at the same time when they see the officer respond to the aggression. Try this yourself. Say the word "hey," and see how you naturally react physically.

When looking at the footwork for this kind of response, the officer is, of course, at a good off-set stance (level 1 of relative positioning) when dealing with the suspect. Because the officer is acutely aware of the potential for physical confrontation, he is up on the balls of his feet, leaning forward. The rear foot gives a "push off," generating the force in the response. The feet then move forward to intercept the suspect and to apply the technique (Figures 3.1 and 3.2).

Figure 3.1 The pre-emptive footwork.

Figure 3.2 The pre-emptive footwork; notice how the body shifts forward.

In Figures 3.1 and 3.2, you can observe the footwork associated with the pre-emptive response. The body moves forward, with the lead foot sliding closer to the target, while the rear foot supplies the push (Figure 3.3).

This footwork is enhanced by keeping the knees bent slightly, which allows the body to use the total mass behind any kind of strike being delivered by the body. The whole key to success for this is to have a clear indication that an attack is coming and to meet it with an appropriate response.

Let's take a look at some situations officers may find themselves in, where a suspect has become aggressive.

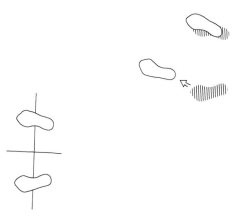

Figure 3.3 Illustration of the pre-emptive footwork.

Response to a Single Grab

The following scenario is presented to provide a clearer understanding of the concept behind the pre-emptive response. The technique itself is not as important as the response and how the body moves and reacts to the threat (Figure 3.4).

Figure 3.4 The suspect reaches out and grabs the officer.

In this example, the suspect has reached out and taken hold of the officer's shirt. Pay attention here to the placement of the feet of the officer, so that when the following photographs are viewed, you can observe how the body moves forward and toward the attack (Figure 3.5).

Figure 3.5 The officer brings the hands up and inside of the attack.

As the officer confronts the threat, he brings his hands to the inside of the attack, moving more inside and, at the same time, taking a step forward to engage with the subject. Notice how by moving the hands to the inside, it moves the arm and hand that is gripping the shirt out of the way and unable to truly respond quickly to what the officer will follow with (Figure 3.6).

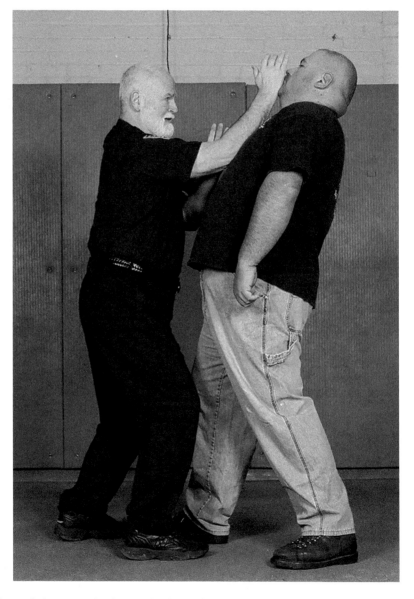

Figure 3.6 Notice the footwork of the officer as the attack is directed to the suspect.

In this example, the officer follows up with a palm strike to the suspect. Notice how the right arm of the officer could very easily move and capture the suspect's left arm if he were to bring that into the fight. By moving into the attack, the officer is able to neutralize some of the suspect's weapons and is able to gain control of the situation.

Response to a Two-Hand Grab

If a suspect is willing to reach out and grab an officer, he will, in many cases, do so with both hands. This is a more powerful attack, because in order to carry this out, the suspect is bringing his entire body force with him. The officer then must be able to handle that and deal with it effectively (Figure 3.7).

Figure 3.7 Two hand grab attack.

As the suspect begins to make his move, notice how the officer has observed the intentions of the suspect and is already starting to move his body to make an interception of that attack, so that it is not able to land with the full force (Figure 3.8).

Figure 3.8 The officer moves into the attack keeping the arms inside of the attack.

The officer brings his hands up and counters the suspect's hands. Notice again how the officer is stepping into the attack, moving forward. The arms and hands of the officer push down and out on the suspect's arms and hands, deflecting the attack. Keep in mind that the suspect will be moving forward, and it is very difficult to change directions within the time frame of the officer's response (Figure 3.9).

In this example, the officer follows up with a forearm strike to the head. Notice how the suspect's primary weapons, his hands, have been effectively neutralized and pushed to the outside of the fight at this point. The officer is also in close now, so the ability of the suspect to apply his legs as a response

Figure 3.9 Bring on the inside provides options for follow-up technique.

is limited. Here, the officer can then follow up with a technique to take the suspect into a position where he can be controlled.

Response to a Punch

The same principle applies when the attack is a punch that is coming toward the officer. The footwork carries the officer into the attack and this provides the officer with the opportunities to overcome the aggression. A punch being thrown, of course, shows even more aggression on the part of a suspect, as he is willing to take his attack to a more violent level (Figure 3.10).

Figure 3.10 Strong arm strike attack.

In this example, the officer has "read" the suspect and realizes that a punch is imminent. Notice how the officer is in a fighting stance, with hands up to protect the head. When it comes to protecting against a punch, if you have your hands up in front, there is little room for a punch to get through. This is why, it is critical to keep your hands up in a fight (Figure 3.11).

Figure 3.11 Moving into the attack the officer launches a response.

In response to the attack, the officer moves forward. Again, notice the placement of the feet in Figure 3.11. Also pay attention to how the officer has lowered his center of gravity and his knees, which take him out of the path of the attacking arm and again on the inside of the attack. Here, the office initiates a forearm strike to the side of the head, keeping his other hand close to his face to deflect a possible counterattack (Figure 3.12).

The force of the officer's attack will push the subject back and away from the officer. Notice how the officer is in position to move forward to gain control of the subject and has a very stable posture.

Figure 3.12 This places the officer in a good position for follow-up techniques.

Response to a Kick

The kick is a more powerful attack, because the weapon is larger and can carry more impact. However, the response from the officer will be the same, moving toward the attack. In these examples, notice that if you are observant and can detect the intentions of a suspect, how much more effective your response can be. This is why, it is critical to pay attention to your surroundings and the people you are encountering on the street.

Here, the officer has "read" the suspect and noticed that a kick is coming in. Take a moment though and look at the suspect's body (Figure 3.13).

Figure 3.13 A kick attack.

Notice that the way in which the body has to move to deliver a kick also telegraphs the intention to kick. This is vital information when split seconds matter. Here, the officer is raising his foot to deliver an attack of his own (Figure 3.14).

Figure 3.14 The officer brings the lead leg up to meet the kick.

In response to the attack, the officer uses his leg to attack the incoming leg. Notice how by doing this the officer does not have to deal with any of the other weapons that the suspect can bring to the fight at this point. This attack also neutralizes the incoming leg before it can do any damage to the officer (Figure 3.15).

The force of the officer's kick will naturally send the suspect's leg backward. Notice how this turns the suspect's body and how the officer can easily follow up by moving in and gaining control of the suspect. This again is all possible because the officer moved to the attack and so placed himself in a position to deal effectively with the threat.

Figure 3.15 The response moves the suspect back and places the officer in a position for follow up.

Response with an Impact Weapon

Officers have many tools that they carry and utilize every day on the job. The impact weapon is one of the more commonly used tools. This can come in many forms, from a standard baton to a collapsible baton to even a flashlight. Since these tools are often in the hands of officers during a confrontation, being able to utilize them, along with appropriate technique and application, can help diffuse a confrontation more quickly. In the last example, we will take a look at the use of an impact weapon and the pre-emptive response (Figure 3.16).

Figure 3.16 Response to threat with an impact weapon.

Here, the officer is utilizing the flashlight during an encounter with a subject. Notice how the officer keeps his free hand up during the situation, to be able to react quickly, if necessary. Pay attention to the suspect's body position—what is it telling you? (Figure 3.17).

Figure 3.17 The officer responds to the attack by moving toward it and pressing the impact tool against the suspect's shoulder.

Here, the suspect advances on the officer. Realizing the attack, the officer moves toward the attack. Notice the position of the feet and the bent knees. Using the impact weapon, the officer presses into the opposite shoulder of the suspect. Notice how this pressure begins to change the movement of the suspect (Figure 3.18).

If the suspect continues to present a threat, then the officer is in a position for a follow-up response. In this one, the officer uses the impact weapon to move the head upward, changing the direction of the suspect's body. Notice how the officer is in a position to take control of the suspect, and the opportunity for the suspect to respond is limited at this point.

The success of the pre-emptive response relies on moving into the attack. As was mentioned before, this is what most police defensive tactics programs

Figure 3.18 The response can continue if the suspect continues to struggle by moving the response to the head changing the direction of the suspect's body.

are designed to do. Performed correctly, this is also why the techniques in these programs are very effective. However, think about this. Is the person that you are encountering on the street someone you feel comfortable getting close to? If not, then this is why many good techniques designed to defeat an attack fail, because, in order to carry out a pre-emptive attack, you must be willing to get close to the suspect and get inside of their attack. Although many officers utilize this kind of response to an attack throughout their career, not all officers feel as confident in every situation. In order to still accomplish the mission of enforcing the law, more responses are needed. We must provide officers the flexibility to deal with the threat that they face in the most efficient manner for them—which means getting the mind and body on the same page.

The Strategic Response

4

Be like water making its way through cracks. Do not be assertive, but adjust to the object, and you shall find a way round or through it. If nothing within you stays rigid, outward things will disclose themselves.

Empty your mind, be formless. Shapeless, like water. If you put water into a cup, it becomes the cup. You put water into a bottle and it becomes the bottle. You put it in a teapot it becomes the teapot. Now, water can flow or it can crash. Be water my friend.

—Bruce Lee
Bruce Lee Jeet Kune Do, 1977

The strategic response to an attack is designed to give the officer time to draw out the attack. This provides the opportunity to strike back, once an opponent has extended himself. Here, the officer observes the attack moving in his direction. The first thing is to get out of the way of the attack. If done right, this gives the officer the opening to direct his counterattack and gain control of the subject. The concept here is to allow the officer to look for an advantage or opportunity to move into the attacker, specifically, when the time and opportunity are there.

Perhaps, a better illustration of this approach might be found in the game of chess. The knight in chess is a unique piece, because it can attack in an unorthodox manner. It moves one space in one direction and then two in another, sort of in the shape of the letter L. This enables the knight to avoid many straight-line attacks and allows it to attack at an angle that gives it an advantage over other pieces in the game (Figure 4.1).

This same idea will allow an officer the chance to escape the initial attack and will give him the ability to respond to the attack from a more tactically advantageous position. In the strategic response, the officer moves backward in an angle that takes him out of the range of the suspect's weapons, yet close enough to return to the fight. There is an instinct within all of us that makes us want to move away from danger. By allowing your body to go in the direction it wants to, but with the added tactical advantage of moving in a 45-degree angle, officers will find themselves in a more defensible position— one that allows them those extra moments needed to mentally catch up in

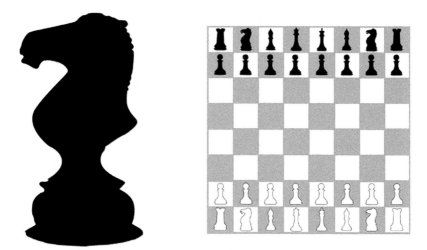

Figure 4.1 The strategic response is like a knight in the game of chess. (Courtesy of pixabay.com.)

the fight. Staying with responses that go with natural instincts increases their effectiveness. Under stress, individuals revert to their survival instincts, and it is always better to work with yourself than work against yourself.

Moving back in a 45-degree angle has another advantage. During the stress of an actual attack, techniques are often reversed. For example, most training is conducted utilizing the strong side, and as long as officers can perform the task with this strong side, most trainers will pass them on. However, in the realities of the street and in the frantic microseconds when the assault is launched, classroom perfection is translated into panic reactions. Until the officer can mentally catch up in the fight and remember his training, he will rely on his instinct.

Because this principle works from both sides, it doesn't matter if the officer steps back with his right foot or his left foot, as long as he moves back in a 45-degree angle, away from the assault. Once gaining this tactical advantage, his mental processes will be up to speed. At that point, all of the techniques learned in training will come to mind and the proper force option can be applied.

A verbal response to help illustrate this feeling would be to say the words, "hold it." This creates a picture of someone holding up their hands and trying to get the other person to pause or stop. In this response, the officer is doing just that by moving back from the attack, yet still in control of the situation. Verbally telling someone to hold it or back off provides a warning that their actions are uncalled for and will result in an action that they will not like.

The footwork here in the strategic response is critical for the success of the movement. Even with an officer standing in a good offset stance, the officer's movements must be back and away from the subject in a 45-degree angle. If the officer were to move just straight back, the attack could still reach him. It is this movement back and off to the side, much like a knight moving in the game of chess, that gives the officer the ability to first move out of harm's way. If the attacker cannot touch the officer, then the officer maintains control, as he can resort to another weapon if the situation calls for it. However, if it is going to remain an empty-hands situation, then the officer can respond to the attack by moving into the suspect, once the attacker has extended himself. The officer must move out of alignment with the suspect and will have the opportunity and timing to use his techniques in response (Figure 4.2a and b).

(a)   (b)

Figure 4.2 (a and b) Illustrate the footwork for the strategic response.

Figure 4.2 show how the body moves back and away from an attack. Notice how the back foot slides back and away, allowing the officer to lower his body to a more stable fighting stance, and keeps his distance from the assault.

Remember that with this approach, if you follow a straight line, moving backward, you are still within the range of the suspect's reach. The reason for this is simple logic. When a person throws a punch, the direction of the attack is aimed at where you are at the moment the punch is launched. If you step straight back, this will not prevent you from the threat, as all that the attacker has to do is to lean a little further for the punch to reach its target. That is why, the backward angle is so effective; their reach is not able to find you.

As with the pre-emptive response, we will take a look at some situations and see how the strategic response could be applied. Again, the actual technique or follow-up is not as important as noting how the officer deals with the situation. Many different techniques could be applied to the threat, but the body movement and its application are the important parts in play. A technique that cannot be applied is of little value, so the officer needs to give himself the best chance for success by working with his body and not against it (Figure 4.3).

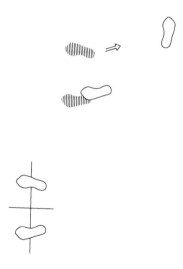

Figure 4.3 Illustration of the footwork for the strategic response.

Response to a Grab

As with pre-emptive, we will look at similar attacks, so that you can contrast the responses with the different approaches.

Here, the officer is in a good offset stance, yet the suspect can easily reach him (Figure 4.4).

Notice the footwork of the officer in Figure 4.4. By moving back from the attack, the officer has taken himself out of the line of the attack.

Figure 4.4 The suspect here is reaching for the officer.

Here, the officer has trapped the incoming hand. Because he is moving back from the attack at an angle and not in a straight line, it draws the suspect out and off balance. Here, the officer has stepped back with the right foot (Figure 4.5).

Figure 4.5 The officer shifts the body back and away from the attack and grabbing the incoming arm.

As the officer deals with the threat, he controls the suspect's hand by bending it at the wrist, while controlling it and working against the nerves in the wrist. The officer then shifts direction (Figure 4.6).

Figure 4.6 By applying a wrist grab to the suspect increases the effectiveness of the response.

After gaining control of the suspect, the officer now steps in a 45-degree angle with his left foot, while controlling the wrist of the suspect. Notice how the officer's feet are placed and how the suspect is not able to gain balance or be in a position to respond to the control technique. From this point, the suspect can be placed on the ground in an armbar, and handcuffs can be applied (Figure 4.7).

Figure 4.7 By moving back and away again the officer is able to move the suspect to the ground.

Response to a Two-Hand Grab

Much like the pre-emptive response, the officer reads the suspect and realizes that an aggressive action is about to happen. In preparation, the officer brings his own hands up, to be engaged in the confrontation (Figures 4.8 and 4.9).

Figure 4.8 The attack is a two-handed grab.

Figure 4.9 The response is to shift back and away from the attack while moving to deal with the incoming threat.

Here, in Figure 4.10, the officer steps back with his left foot, allowing him to skirt the attack and trap the right arm of the suspect. Notice how the officer's body is back from the attack and is turning away from a direct assault (Figure 4.10).

Figure 4.10 By shifting again the officer is able to move from danger into a control hold.

Now, the officer steps back with his right foot, which has now prevented him from any major threat that the suspect can present. The now trapped arm of the suspect can be controlled by applying pressure to the wrist by the officer's hand and forearm (Figure 4.11).

Figure 4.11 shows a close-up of the control technique. Again, remember that the technique is applicable, but by moving in a strategic response, the officer has been able to remove himself from the threat.

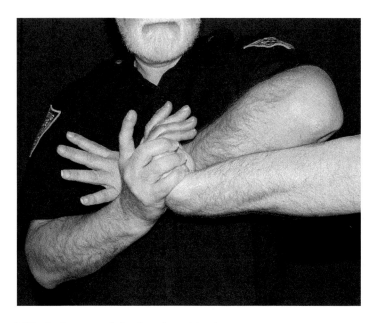

Figure 4.11 A close up of the hand positioning.

Now the officer is able to become offensive, and by using his left foot and moving forward in the 45-degree motion and controlling the arm of the suspect, he is able to place him in an armbar and control the suspect. From this position, the suspect can be moved into a handcuffing position (Figure 4.12).

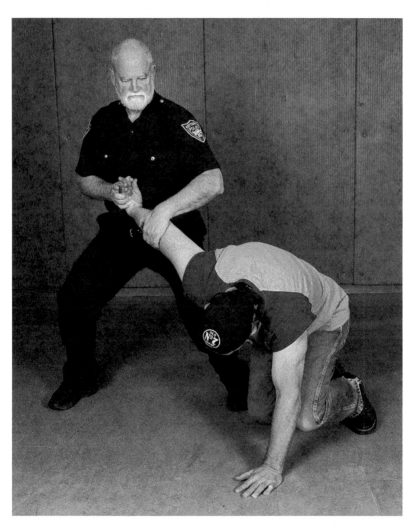

Figure 4.12 The officer can then place the suspect on the ground for handcuffing.

Response to a Punch

Here, both the officer and suspect are in a fighting stance. Now, as you review the strategic response, contrast this with the pre-emptive. Remember that in the pre-emptive, the officer would move into the suspect and meet the punch on the inside, allowing the suspect's punch to go to the outside (Figure 4.13).

Figure 4.13 The attack is a punch.

In the strategic response, the officer will move away from the attack. Be mindful of the footwork (Figure 4.14).

Figure 4.14 By moving back and away the officer is out of harm's way and can respond to the attack.

The officer moves his right foot back and away from the suspect. Notice how this movement allows the officer to be on the outside of the attack and provides a clear target for the officer to engage. By striking the suspect's arm, the officer is able to deliver his own punch, while staying away from the assault (Figure 4.15).

Since we all know that one punch does not usually stop a fight, the suspect will, in all likelihood, engage with his other arm. The officer merely applies the strategic principle again by moving away from the incoming attack (Figure 4.15).

Figure 4.15 If the suspect continues to fight, the officer can shift again moving away from the punch.

By moving his left foot back and away, the officer is again able to move outside of the attack and can again attack the suspect's arm. This motion can continue for as long as the officer needs it, in order to gain control of the situation. Notice how by moving in this fashion, the officer allows the suspect to expose his body, while the officer remains outside of the reach of the suspect. This provides the officer with a tactical advantage and provides him with space, which will allow the officer time to think of options available to him (Figure 4.16).

Figure 4.16 Once out of reach of the punch the officer can respond with a counter strike.

Figure 4.17 illustrates what happens if the officer does not move back and away from the assault but moves in a straight line. The suspect is able to carry out the attack by leaning just a little more and reaching the officer. This cannot be stressed enough: the movement must be back and away from the attack (Figure 4.17).

Figure 4.17 It is critical to move in a 45° angle and not straight back as the suspect's punch will still reach the officer if moving in a straight line.

Response to a Kick

The response to a kick is similar to the punch and grab. The officer will move back with the right foot, which will again take him out of the range of the suspect's leg (Figures 4.18 and 4.19).

Once escaped from the threat, the officer is able to deliver a kick in response. Notice how the suspect's primary weapons, legs and arms, are out of the way and are unable to reach the officer; however, the officer is still in a position to strike back at the suspect.

Figure 4.18 The attack is a kick.

Figure 4.19 By moving away from the incoming kick the officer can launch a counter kick out of the suspect's reach.

Response with an Impact Weapon

As we mentioned in the pre-emptive response examples, officers carry many tools with them on a daily basis. We demonstrated how an officer could use an impact tool such as a flashlight with the pre-emptive approach; we provide you with the same here for the strategic response. The officer in Figure 4.20 sees the threat from the suspect and applies a response based on the strategic response (Figures 4.20 and 4.21).

Here, the officer moves his left foot back and away from the suspect. Notice how this carries him out of the way of the suspect's reach. The officer can then respond to the attack with the impact weapon (Figure 4.22).

Figure 4.20 The response to a threat with an impact weapon.

Figure 4.21 The officer moves away from the threat and can respond with a counter strike to the arm of the suspect.

Figure 4.22 The officer is then in a position to gain control of the suspect.

By shifting the right foot toward the suspect, the officer gains control of the suspect's arm, while, at the same time, moves the flashlight under the arm to gain a better control hold on the suspect. Notice the foot position of the officer and how the knees are bent in a stable position. Compare that with the posture of the suspect (Figure 4.23).

The officer in Figure 4.23 merely shifts back on his left foot. This extends the suspect to the point the officer has control of him and can maneuver him into a handcuffing position. The footwork provides the officer the opportunity to escape an attack and to apply applicable responses to the threat.

When practicing the knight move, officers should check their feet to ensure that they are moving back and at a 45-degree angle. Often, officers step back and to the side, sort of in a reverse T. The problem with this is that it is similar to just stepping back in a straight line. The suspect will be able to adjust, and his attack will be successful. It doesn't take long to learn this simple move, but a few practice steps are needed to ensure that you're moving in the correct way.

As we mentioned with the pre-emptive response, the key to this is to move close to the suspect. Not everyone feels comfortable getting that close to someone who wants to do them harm. The strategic approach provides

Figure 4.23 The officer can then maneuver the suspect into a handcuffing position.

time and space for an officer to deal with aggressive behavior and still remain just outside of the reach from that attack.

In these times of lawsuits, video recordings, and other legal entanglements, officers cannot rely on brute force or weapons to respond to every situation. We all need to become smarter than our opponents and to prepare for their attack in a manner that they will not expect. By moving backward and away in a 45-degree angle and then crashing back into a would-be attacker, an officer will find himself in a better position to take a prisoner to jail and return home to his family.

The Evasive Response 5

Best defense—no be there!

—**Mr. Miyagi**
The Karate Kid, 1984

The evasive response provides the officer the opportunity to not only move away from the threat but also to place himself in a good position to take control of the subject. The technique though is one where the officer will actually move close to the attack as it is coming in but around it—just like two ships passing each other. The attack goes in one direction, while the officer moves alongside it. This vantage point gives the officer an excellent position to gain control and apply a takedown technique to gain compliance.

This is the approach that was discovered by one of the authors while training at the Cincinnati Police Academy. It was demonstrated to him that this was a natural response when faced with a threat. The idea of meeting a threat head-on is not always appealing, and it depends on what that threat is.

Another example of this was demonstrated by Dr. Masaaki Hatsumi, the grandmaster of Ninjutsu, at a training session in Kettering, Ohio, during the 1980s. Dr. Hatsumi was instructing in what he called the "wind" element. He instructed his demonstration assistant to strike him any time he wanted with a punch to his head. He then turned, so that his back was toward this person. When the punch came, Dr. Hatsumi merely shifted his body and head slightly, allowing the punch to slip past his head, missing completely. It appeared as if the person throwing the punch was truly fighting the wind.

Think about the game of football for a moment. The offensive lineman must meet the threat of the defensive lineman and linebackers head-on, because it is the mission to block the incoming attack. When they do their job well, the offense line is able to block or move the defense and the offense can execute their plays to achieve their mission. This would be more like a pre-emptive response and even strategic response, depending on how the offensive lineman blocks the defense. The wide receiver, however, is another story. The wide receiver cannot get caught up in a head-on confrontation with the defensive back, because his mission is to get open to receive a pass. To accomplish this, the receiver needs to move past the defensive back into a position where the pass can be completed. The evasive approach to a threat is similar in that the officer will want to move outside of the threat to accomplish the mission of gaining control of the suspect.

If you think about this approach, think about a situation where you were perhaps facing a friend who was agitated, but who you did not wish to hurt him or you. As your friend moved, perhaps, in an aggressive manner, you would want to move alongside and around him and gain control of him, until he calms down. The same principle applies here. The officer avoids the attack by moving, and then, he finds that he is in a much better position to apply the techniques that he is trained to utilize.

A verbal response to help illustrate this would be to say the word "easy." This is a non-threatening word and conjures up the image of someone trying to calm the situation. Here, the officer can say this word, and it transmits the verbal cue that the officer does not wish to harm the suspect but that he is in control of the situation and he will succeed. Think about that for a moment. If your actions are being recorded, imagine that, on the recording, you hear the officer telling the person "easy," as he moves into a control position, without the suspect being able to connect with his attack.

The footwork with this technique again has the officer in a good offset stance. No matter which side the attack comes in from, the officer moves toward the suspect but just off to suspect's side, or the officer can move back and to the side. This gives the officer the ability to respond to the quickness of the attack, yet, at the same time, to be in a position to deal with it effectively. However, whichever side the officer moves to, he needs to be aware of other possible attacks that the suspect can present, so that the response is rapid because of the proximity of the suspect. Unlike the strategic approach, where the officer can continue to move back and away to stay out of harm's reach, in evasive approach, the officers must keep moving alongside the attack, which also presents their body close to the attack (Figure 5.1a and b).

For the purpose of demonstration, in Figure 5.1a and b, the officer has his hands up. Think of this as someone telling you "easy" and to calm down. From the outside, it appears as the officer is diffusing the situation, and, of course, if that works, then it is better for all. However, in the evasive approach, if the suspect continues with his attack, the officer merely steps to the side (Figure 5.1b) and avoids the incoming attack (Figure 5.2).

(a)   (b)

Figure 5.1 (a and b) Show the footwork for the evasive response.

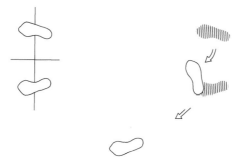

Figure 5.2 This illustration shows the footwork for the evasive response.

The suspect begins to feel like he is fighting the wind, because wherever he launches an attack, the officer has moved out of harm's way.

As with pre-emptive and strategic approaches, we will now examine some responses in the evasive approach. Again, keep in mind that this is only to demonstrate how the approach works, and there are multiple techniques that can be applied to the threat being dealt with. The important point is to understand how the body moves and how it can work with the natural instinct to get out of the way of danger.

Response to a Grab

Here, the suspect (Figure 5.3) reaches out and takes hold of the officer, perhaps bringing his other hand up to throw a punch (Figures 5.3 through 5.5).

Figure 5.3 The attack is a grab.

Figure 5.4 As the attack comes in the officer begins to move to the side and away from the attack.

Figure 5.5 The officer moves his right leg to the side of the suspect while gripping the left arm of the suspect and engaging the head.

In response, the officer moves his right leg to the side of the suspect, while gripping the left arm of the suspect and engaging the head. Notice the suspect's natural reaction to shift to the right and to be a little off center, and the officer is in a position of control (Figure 5.6).

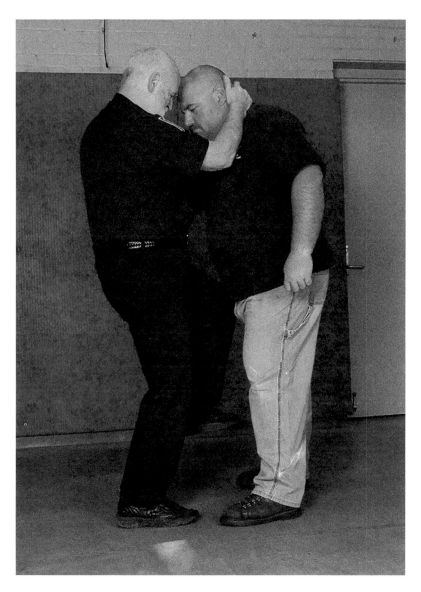

Figure 5.6 A possible follow-up move from this position, the officer could move quickly to a knee strike.

A possible follow-up move from this position is that the officer could move quickly to a knee strike, as he was already gaining the middle ground and the suspect's primary weapons were moved out of the confrontation (Figure 5.7).

By stepping back and away from the suspect, the officer can now place him in an armbar and then move him to a takedown position and follow with handcuffing.

Figure 5.7 Moving back the suspect can be positioned for handcuffing.

Response to a Two-Hand Grab

As the suspect moves in with both hands, the officer begins to deflect with his own hands, while beginning to move away from the pending attack. Notice the subtle shift in weight and footwork, as we progress through this example (Figures 5.8 and 5.9).

Figure 5.8 The attack is a two-hand grab.

Figure 5.9 The officer counters the arms of the suspect by moving one high and one low. The officer begins to move to the side of the attack.

The officer counters the arms of the suspect by moving one high and one low. The officer begins to move to the side of the attack (Figure 5.10).

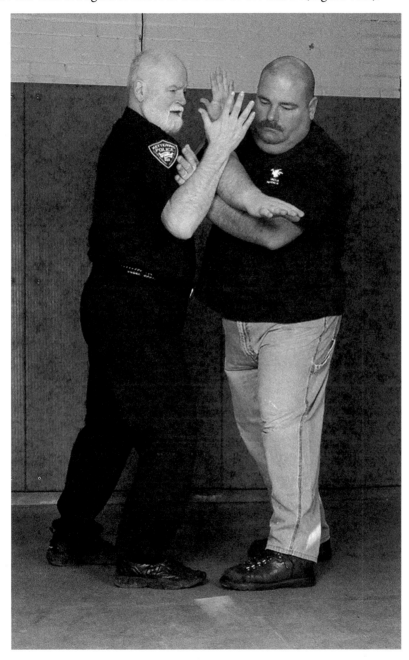

Figure 5.10 By moving to the side in the evasive approach, the officer traps the arms of the suspect.

By moving to the side in the evasive approach, the officer traps the arms of the suspect (Figure 5.11).

Figure 5.11 shows a close-up of how the officer utilizes his arms to trap and control both of the suspect's arms with basically one arm.

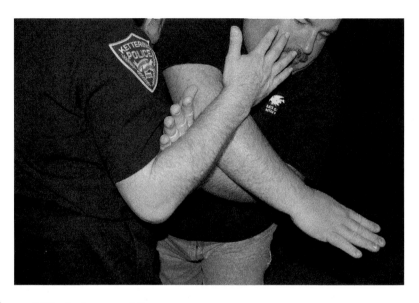

Figure 5.11 A close up of the arms.

Note how the left hand is trapped under the right arm on the suspect. This controls both weapons, while the officer still has a free hand to work with (Figure 5.12).

Figure 5.12 The officer can the move into a control technique.

The officer begins to move his free hand behind the suspect to take him to the ground for control and follow-up. Notice how the suspect has no real opportunity to utilize any of his main weapons at this point (Figure 5.13).

By lowering his body weight, the officer can execute a throw, take the suspect to the ground, and then move to a handcuffing position.

Figure 5.13 By lowering his body weight the officer can execute a throw and take the suspect to the ground and then move to a handcuffing position.

Response to a Punch

Here, we have a suspect who intend to throw a punch at the officer. Just imagine here that the officer is saying "easy" to the suspect (Figures 5.14 and 5.15).

Figure 5.14 The attack is a punch.

Figure 5.15 The officer moves to the outside of the punch while moving his right arm underneath the attack.

The officer moves to the outside of the punch, while moving his right arm underneath the attack. By moving to the outside, there is no chance that the suspect can bring any other weapons into the conflict. The officer has isolated the primary threat and, at the same time, moved to a position to the side of the suspect and out of harm's way (Figure 5.16).

As the officer moves in, he brings his arms up and around the suspect. Take note of how the suspect is not in a position to respond to the move by the officer. The officer is in control of the suspect at this point. However, keep in mind that, as was mentioned at the beginning of the chapter, think of this as

Figure 5.16 As the officer moves in, he brings his arms up and around the suspect.

if it were someone you knew whom you didn't want to hurt, yet you couldn't allow him to hurt you. By controlling him in the evasive approach, you would be the one in control of how the conflict moved forward (Figure 5.17).

Figure 5.17 With the suspect's shoulder and head isolated and between the officer's arms he can be moved to the ground for follow-up action to move him to a handcuffing position.

With the suspect's shoulder and head isolated and between the officer's arms, he can be moved to the ground for follow-up action to move him to a handcuffing position.

Response to a Kick

As the officer observes that the suspect has begun to launch his kick, the officer starts to move out of the way. Notice how, in this example, the officer is merely picking up his foot and will shift his body out of the way of the kick, setting up the response (Figures 5.18 and 5.19).

Figure 5.18 The attack is a kick.

Figure 5.19 The officer moves his whole body out of the way of the attack.

The officer moves his whole body out of the way of the attack. Notice how this move also sets him up for a counterkick. Look at the body's position of the two, and notice who is in the better position to carry the fight forward (Figure 5.20).

Here, the officer delivers a counterkick, driving the suspect's leg back. From here, the officer is in a good position to move to a control hold and effect an arrest.

Figure 5.20 Here the officer delivers a counter kick driving the suspect's leg back.

Response with an Impact Weapon

In this example, the suspect is reaching out to grab the officer. The officer is holding a flashlight and begins to shift to the outside of the incoming attack (Figures 5.21 and 5.22).

By utilizing the evasive approach and moving to the outside of the attack, the officer can counter with the impact tool and gain control of the situation.

The evasive approach provides the opportunity to get outside of an incoming attack, yet remaining close enough to the threat to effectively deal with it. This evasive approach works with the body's natural instinct to move away from danger and still provides an officer the ability to maintain control over a hostile threat.

Figure 5.21 The response to a threat with an impact weapon.

Figure 5.22 By utilizing the evasive approach and moving to the outside of the attack, the officer can counter with the impact tool and gain control of the situation.

The Grounding
Response

6

Aspire to be like Mt. Fuji, with such a broad and solid foundation that the strongest earthquake cannot move you, and so tall that the greatest enterprises of common men seem insignificant from your lofty perspective. With your mind as high as Mt Fuji you can see all things clearly. And you can see all the forces that shape events; not just the things happening near to you.

—Miyamoto Musashi
A Book of Five Rings, 1645

Much of what has been disclosed to this point will enhance an officer's abilities when faced with opponents who pose more of a threat to them. The strategic and evasive approaches will be especially effective for an officer in the David-versus-Goliath type of situation. Officers smaller in stature or those who find that they are facing a more skilled opponent may find these responses to be of most use. However, what if an officer finds himself in the position of being Goliath to David? The litigation of use-of-force cases presents an interesting dilemma for the officer, because too much force will cause bystanders to perhaps criticize the officer and say that the officer was abusive. The Goliath-versus-David situation presents another dynamic, which is the call for the grounded response. What if, for example, an officer was faced with a much smaller suspect who clearly posed no threat but responded to the person's actions with the techniques mentioned in the pre-emptive chapter? The officer would be well within his general orders, because it would be covered by the techniques taught, but the image it would project to the public would be one of questionable force. Having an alternative way to deal with such an encounter could diffuse the situation and allow the officer and offender a better alternative.

A verbal response that an officer might use is "stop it." This is an authoritative tone and speaks to what the officer is experiencing. The attack to the officer is more of a nuisance, just like a child attacking an adult. The attack must be dealt with, but it can be swept away. No attack can get past the officer here, yet the officer needs to be conscious of his position and respond with the

95

force necessary to diffuse the attack and not overdo it. This is the key—not to use more force than necessary to deal with the threat.

The footwork here finds the officer on solid ground, again in a good off-set stance. However, the body weight of the officer is centered, and this provides him a solid base from which to receive and deal with the threat as it approaches (Figures 6.1a and 6.1b).

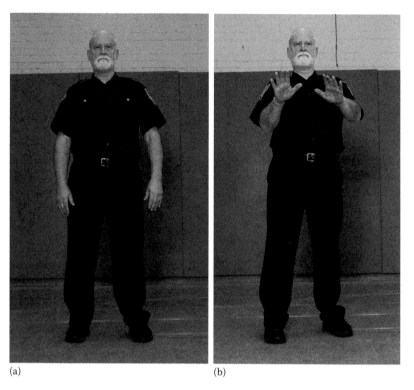

(a)   (b)

Figure 6.1 (a and b) Show the footwork for the grounding response.

Here, the grounding approach is demonstrated with solid footing. The footwork is merely a slight shift of the foot, moving the center of gravity slightly to deal with the incoming threat (Figure 6.2).

Figure 6.2 will perhaps give a more detailed look at the grounding footwork.

As we did with pre-emptive, strategic, and evasive approaches, we will examine the same situations but apply the grounding approach to see the results. This again is working with the body in a situation where a threat is present, but the officer is completely confident that he can deal with it. However, here is something to keep in mind: during any confrontation, things can change and can change quickly. A situation that you may feel is completely in control can move in a different direction. By understanding these four approaches, the officer can move from approach to approach, depending on how the encounter is progressing. Do not get trapped in the idea that these approaches are static, and once you begin with one approach, you must stay with that. Any fight is a fluid situation, and as a result, more options open to an officer working with his natural tendencies increase his chance for success. As the saying goes—keep you options open—in a fight you may want them! Now, let's take a look at the grounding approach.

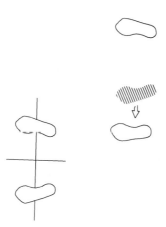

Figure 6.2 An illustration of the footwork for the grounding response.

Response to a Grab

As we progress through the grab response, notice how the officer does not overreact but merely shifts his weight slightly and applies an appropriate response to the threat, dealing with it in a manner that controls the situation (Figures 6.3 and 6.4).

Figure 6.3 The attack is a grab.

Figure 6.4 As the grab comes in, the officer moves it to the outside while bringing his hand up to control the subject.

As the grab comes in, the officer moves it to the outside, while bringing his hand up to control the subject. By moving his fingers to the eyes, he creates a distraction to misdirect the suspect (Figure 6.5).

Figure 6.5 The officer now shifts slightly while applying a control move on the right arm of the suspect.

The officer now shifts slightly, while applying a control move on the right arm of the suspect (Figure 6.6).

Figure 6.6 The officer, now in control of the suspect, begins to move him to the ground.

The officer, now in control of the suspect, begins to move him to the ground (Figure 6.7).

From here, the suspect can be moved to a handcuffing position. The officer maintained control of the threat, yet made little movement offensively. As an outside observer, if you saw this on the street, what would be your thoughts on how the officer handled the threat?

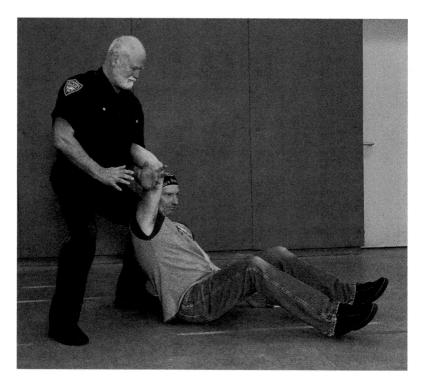

Figure 6.7 From here the suspect can be moved to a handcuffing position.

Response from Two-Hand Grab

As you look at the next sequence of photographs, depicting a two-hand grab threat, pay attention to the officer's feet and the movement to deal with the attack (Figures 6.8 and 6.9).

Figure 6.8 The attack is a two-handed grab.

Figure 6.9 Here the officer brings his hands up to diffuse the incoming reach of the suspect.

Notice how stable the officer appears by shifting the foot and center of gravity slightly. In the example the officer brings his hands up to diffuse the incoming reach of the suspect (Figure 6.10).

Figure 6.10 With another slight shift forward the officer is now able to move to an armbar at the same time distracting the suspect with fingers to the head, turning it slightly.

With another slight shift forward, the officer is now able to move to an armbar at the same time, distracting the suspect with fingers to the head, turning it slightly (Figures 6.11 and 6.12).

The suspect is then taken to the ground, while the officer is in a position to apply follow-up techniques and move to handcuffing the suspect.

Figure 6.11 The officer moves in to control the suspect.

Figure 6.12 The suspect is taken to the ground for handcuffing.

Response to a Punch

As you walk through Figures 6.13 through 6.16, notice how the officer deals with the incoming punch. By merely moving his left arm to the side of his face and shifting slightly, he takes himself out of the initial attack. When it comes to defending against an attack, the only area you need to consider is

Figure 6.13 The attack is a punch

your body. You place your hands up, in front of your face, and you will see how easily it is to protect your head. All you need to do is to move the hands slightly in one way or the other to cover. There is no need to overrespond to a threat (Figures 6.13 and 6.14).

Figure 6.14 The officer deflects the punch to the outside.

After dealing with the initial threat, and before the suspect can launch a counterstrike with his left arm, Figures 6.15 and 6.16 show the officer's response by moving in and then behind the suspect to take control (Figures 6.15 and 6.16).

Figure 6.15 The officer can then launch a counter strike.

Figure 6.16 The officer can move into a control position.

Response to a Kick

The grounded approach in dealing with a kick is demonstrated in Figures 6.17 and 6.18. As the kick begins to move toward the officer, the response is to counter with a kick of his own. This stops the aggressive movement, and then, the officer can move to another technique to gain control of the subject. Again, with the grounded approach, the officer feels completely in control and confident that he can deal with the threat (Figures 6.17 and 6.18).

Figure 6.17 The attack is a kick.

Figure 6.18 The officer responds by launching a counter strike.

Response with an Impact Weapon

The response in the grounded approach with an impact weapon is to deal with the threat directly but not in an overaggressive manner. The approach relies in the confidence of the officer and the actions of the suspect. Figures 6.19 through 6.21 demonstrate a possible response of an officer using an impact tool to a suspect. Notice how little the officer moves and how he is able to deal with the incoming threat in a commanding way (Figures 6.19 through 6.21).

Figure 6.19 The response to a threat with an impact weapon.

When you observe the actions of the officer and then think of citizens who are observing this, what kind of impression on use of force would this leave? The officer does not move in an aggressive manner but allows the suspect to bring the attack to him, and he merely deals with what is presented.

The thought and approach of going with the natural tendencies of bodies are a method to enhance the abilities of officers on the street. When we attempt to perform a task that we are unsure of or face a threat that we do not want to meet head-on, having alternatives provides an

Figure 6.20 The officer uses the impact weapon on the back of the suspect's hand.

Figure 6.21 If the suspect continues to struggle the officer can respond further.

opportunity for success for the officers as well as for the public they serve. Each approach offers options, depending on the threat that you are facing and your level of confidence. Some officers may never need to utilize an evasive or strategic response, while others may make those their main options. All officers come in different sizes and skill levels and bring different abilities. However, they are all expected to accomplish the mission assigned to them. How they accomplish that mission depends on them. By going with their natural tendencies and the skills that they have acquired, there is a better chance that the mission will be accomplished in an efficient manner.

Ground Fighting

7

It's not whether you get knocked down, it's whether you get up.

—Vince Lombardi
Motivation Lombardi Style, 1992

Anyone who has been involved in a police-suspect physical encounter will tell you that there is a very high probability that, eventually, the fight will fall to the ground. Understanding some key principles can make a difference in such a fight. There are, of course, more restrictions and fewer options available to you because of the nature of being on the ground, but this does not mean that you are limited to only a few defensive techniques. As in any fight, when you are standing or are on the ground, the most important thing is to keep your head about you and to note your options and openings as quickly as you can.

Before even thinking of going to the ground, you should first think about your gun belt. The reason why you would want to look at your gun belt is because as an officer, you will carry many items on it these days. You will have the gun, ammo cases, handcuffs (sometimes, multiple pairs), taser, collapsible baton, and, perhaps, even pepper spray and a utility knife. When officers place so many items on their belt, it can get to the point that there is very little space between the items. This is especially true for officers with small waists. When you look at the belt, take a moment and consider what would happen if you fell backward on the ground with force. What items are located at the back of the belt and what part of your body are they going to impact? For example, think about the small of your back and how the spine can be vulnerable to injury there. If you have an item that gives very little or is hard and solid, say a handcuff case complete with metal handcuffs, then the potential for injury to your spine and lower back will increase. The force of being pushed to the ground will multiply because of those tools on the belt. So, the first thing to consider is how you place your tools on your belt and where they are located in relation to vulnerable areas on your body.

Once you have made your belt more operational, thinking of the possibility of going to the ground, you will want to know how to go to the ground. Many injuries are caused every year by falls. There is a reason for this, as many of us do not know how to fall to avoid injury. For many of us, our first reaction is to stick our arm out and let that limb take the brunt of the force and weight of our body.

The result can be anything from a sprain to a broken arm. In the middle of a police-suspect encounter, injury to the officer must be reduced as much as possible, in order for the officer to deal with the threat and overcome it.

When it comes to falling backward, the key is to roll yourself into a ball as best you can. Think about a ball for a moment. When it lands on the ground, the force is dispersed because the ball rolls, and not just one part takes all of the energy. Same is the case with the human body. As you feel yourself falling, instead of keeping your body rigid or sticking your arms out to break your fall, draw your arms in, curl your back and try to become like a ball as much as you can. Another point here is to tuck your head, which will reduce the risk of injuring your skull.

In order to be able to accomplish this—of course, it is good to practice— start from a squatting position, so that you can get the feel and form of the movement. As you gain control and confidence, you can move to a higher or standing position. You should, of course, practice on a mat or other soft surface to reduce the risk of injury. The following illustrations demonstrate the technique (Figures 7.1 and 7.2).

Figure 7.1 The practice falling backward start in a squatting position.

Figure 7.2 Fall backward but curl the back so that the head does not hit the ground, the feet and hands are up to face a threat.

When it comes to being pushed from behind or falling forward, the ability to roll and diffuse the energy is an option but an alternative can be found by using your arms to break the fall. Here again, doing a straight arm to try and break your fall will only result in injury to your arm. Keeping your head safe is important, and at the same time, you want to be able to break the fall and cause the least amount of damage to you as possible. The way to accomplish this is to use your forearms. Rather than resisting the force moving you to the ground by trying to drop a knee or some other move, which will most likely injure some part of your body, just allow yourself to fall. Bring your arms up in a 90-degree angle, cup your hands, and allow the muscular part of your arms to absorb the impact. By doing this, your elbows remain out of the way and reduce the chance of injury; this also prevents your head from striking the ground.

The following illustrations will demonstrate this. As with the previous example, start from a low position such as kneeling and work your way up to a higher position to get acquainted with the feel of the technique. Be sure to start this on a soft surface, so that you can do repetitions until you have developed confidence in the motion (Figures 7.3 and 7.4).

Landing on the ground safely during a physical encounter is the first part. Ideally, you will be able to get back to a standing position as quickly as possible before the suspect or suspects can close in on you. If you are pushed from the front and are falling backward, you can turn your fall into a roll

Figure 7.3 To practice falling forward kneel, hold your arms up in front, and cup your hands.

Figure 7.4 Fall forward and allow the arms to cushion the fall.

and roll into a position where you can get back onto your feet fairly quickly. To get back up, you roll forward, placing one leg under you, while rocking up on the other. In this motion, you are able to keep your hands up and face any possible threat that you see.

The move for falling forward is not as smooth as you will need to break the fall with your forearms and then quickly move to one side or the other and gain your feet under you. Staying on your feet gives you the advantage of being able to retreat, gain distance, and utilize the tools on your belt.

If you find yourself on the ground and need to get back on your feet quickly, but a suspect is closing in on you, begin to roll to the side and get your arm in a 90-degree angle, so that when your hand lands on the ground, you can use this arm to provide some space between you and the oncoming aggressor. From there, push yourself upward, using the suspect if you need to, and get back on your feet to face the threat (Figures 7.5 through 7.7).

However, it may not always be possible to get back on your feet. If the attacker is not on top of you already, there are options that you can use from the ground to keep the suspect at bay.

If you find yourself on the ground on your back, you can still get to your tools on the belt. Here, again, is a reason to plan out where you place your tools on the belt. Anything that is behind you on your back will

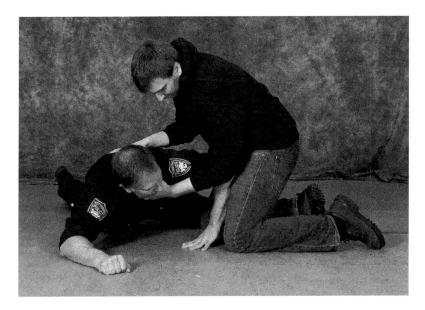

Figure 7.5 To get up from the ground when you are face down is use your elbow to provide space.

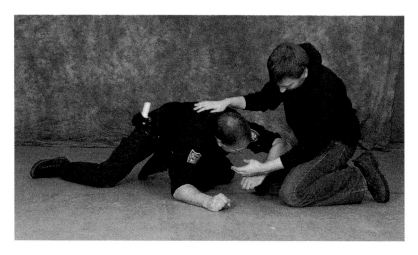

Figure 7.6 Shift the body and use the arm to assist in gaining a standing positon.

Figure 7.7 Gaining a more solid position the officer can better respond to the threat.

obviously be inaccessible in the ground position. The tools on the front and sides will be accessible. Here, you can draw your primary weapon, utilize the taser or pepper spray, for example, or, possibly, even use a collapsible baton. Being able to utilize these weapons will allow you to defend yourself (Figure 7.8).

You can also make use of your hands and feet. However, think about this; on the ground, you can use all four limbs at the same time. When you are standing, this is not possible, but because you are on your back, you can use them. Not only can you use all of your limbs, but you can also move while on your back. If you place one foot on the ground, you can spin around in a circle to face your attacker(s) and bring your other limbs and weapons into a position to defend you. Even if they try to run around and gain an advantage on you, by spinning on your back, powered by your leg, you can move faster than they can and be able to hold your defensive position.

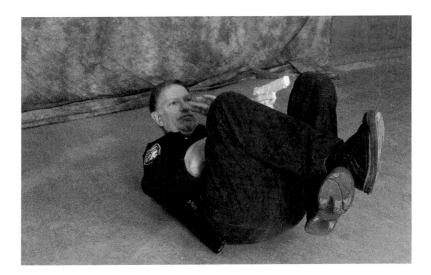

Figure 7.8 On the back the officer can utilize the weapons they hold such as their firearm.

The following illustrations will demonstrate how this is accomplished. Notice how you are able to protect your spine from injury and face your attacker even while on the ground (Figures 7.9 through 7.11).

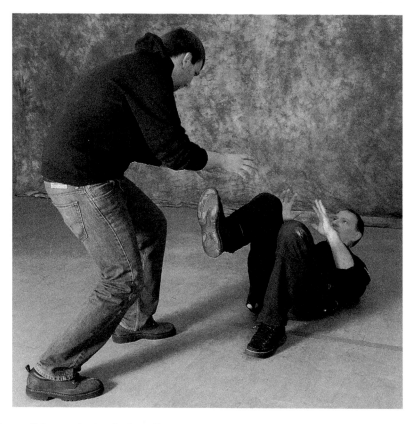

Figure 7.9 On the back the officer can use legs and hands to fend off an attack.

Figure 7.10 By using one foot on the ground the officer can shift on the ground to face the incoming threat.

Figure 7.11 The officer can actually move faster because they are moving in a tighter arc than the suspect.

If you find yourself on the ground, facing forward, and your attacker is on top of you, there is a way to gain the advantage and get him off. Take one of your arms and place it straight out above your body. Take your other arm and place it palm down on the ground in a 90-degree angle. Then, using your straight arm as a fulcrum, you merely push with your arm in the 90-degree angle and move the attacker off of you, as illustrated in Figures 7.12 through 7.14.

However, if you find yourself on the ground and the attacker is on you, then the question would be: do the pre-emptive, strategic, evasive, and grounded approaches still apply? The answer is: yes, the principles of body movement do apply. Now, because you are on the ground, there is limited mobility, but you can still apply the same body movement to deal with an incoming threat.

Figure 7.12 With a suspect on top, the officer moves one arm straight out to form a fulcrum.

Figure 7.13 The other arm then is used to push against the ground.

Figure 7.14 The officer can then move the suspect off and respond with a counterstrike.

Pre-Emptive Response

With the pre-emptive approach, the fight is taken to the threat. On your back, with a suspect on top, you may not have the ability to step into the attack, but you can still apply the same principle. The following photographs show how the officer is still able to take the action directly against the suspect by using both hands and feet to accomplish this (Figures 7.15 through 7.19).

As the officer gains control of the subject, the roles become reversed, and the officer is now in a more controlled position. With the pre-emptive approach, the officer is still able to take direct action against an attack, even on the ground.

Figure 7.15 The pre-emptive response from the ground with the suspect on top.

Figure 7.16 Much like dealing with a threat while standing, the officer moves into the attack.

Figure 7.17 Trapping the suspect's head and legs the officer begins to exert control.

Figure 7.18 The officer immobilizes the suspect.

Figure 7.19 The officer moves to the top position.

Strategic Response

With the strategic response, in the standing position, an officer was able to move back and away from an incoming attack. The motion is very similar to that of the ocean, as it rolls in only to come crashing back on shore. With the strategic approach, the officer did drop back and then crash back in to deal with the suspect. On the ground, of course, there is limited ability to get out of the way completely compared with what an officer has while standing, but it is possible to deflect the attack and then reengage.

The following photographs will illustrate how the strategic approach can be applied in a grounded fighting situation. Notice how the officer shifts his body at the incoming threat and then is able to respond by using his own weapons to disable the suspect (Figures 7.20 through 7.22).

Figure 7.20 The strategic response from the ground.

Figure 7.21 The officer shifts away from the attack.

Figure 7.22 The officer then launches a counter strike.

Grounded Response

In the grounded response, the officer was in the position of controlling the threat from the outset. The response was to brush aside the assault and then to deal with the suspect directly. This principle again can be applied to someone on the ground. The officer can deal with the threat directly, as the following photographs will illustrate. Notice how this form of dealing with the threat is different than the pre-emptive, where the officer took the fight to the suspect. In the grounded approach, the officer deals with the immediate threat and then moves into a position of control (Figures 7.23 through 7.26).

Figure 7.23 Grounded response from the ground.

Figure 7.24 The officer draws the suspect in and counters the attack.

Figure 7.25 The officer then shifts to move the suspect.

Figure 7.26 With the suspect off to the side the officer can gain control.

Evasive Response

In the evasive approach, the principle was to slip past the attack and then deal with the threat from a position of advantage. If an officer is on his back, he will not be able to slip past the attack, like he could do when standing. However, the principle is still sound, and the officer can shift away from the attack and then respond to the threat. The following photographs demonstrate how this principle can be applied. Pay attention to the officer as he shifts away from the incoming attack and is able to get into a position of control. Just as in the standing form of the approach, on the ground, the officer can still evade the attack (Figures 7.27 through 7.30).

Figure 7.27 The evasive response from the ground.

Figure 7.28 The officer moves away from the incoming attack.

Figure 7.29 The officer can now begin to gain control of the suspect.

Figure 7.30 The suspect's weapons are neutralized and the officer has gained control.

Fighting from the ground is not the most advantageous position for an officer. Getting back on your feet is the best course of action. However, in those times when this is not possible and you are faced with a threat, the same principles that apply when you are standing can work to your advantage on the ground. Their application may look a bit different, but the movement of the body will still accomplish the same outcome.

Edged Weapons

8

The more you sweat in training, the less you will bleed in battle.

—Motto of Navy Seals

One of the items officers carry with them in some form or fashion is a knife. This tool has been used from cutting seat belts to cutting bandages to almost anything that you can imagine. It is thought of as a tool, but it can also serve as a weapon, if the situation calls for it. As with any weapon at the disposal of an officer, he or she, must be aware of when it is appropriate to deploy it. However, when it comes to the use of a knife, it rises to the very top of the force continuum, right beside that of a firearm, and is meant to be used only in a deadly force situation.

The same mindset needs to be present in an officer when he would pull a knife as when he would use his sidearm or utilize a rifle or a shotgun. The knife is not a lesser weapon just because it cannot be sent at great distances, but it can be just as effective as a firearm when used in its range. Because officers carry a knife, there may be a situation where a knife will be the only weapon that they can get to, and because of this, they need to be aware of its capabilities.

In 1983, Sergeant Dennis Tueller of the Salt Lake City Police Department in Utah published the results of a test that he conducted on how much distance is a safe distance for officers to be able to pull their gun and fire at someone attacking them with a knife. During his research, he found that a person with a knife can cover 21 feet in 1.5 seconds. This then became a standard that went across the U.S. law enforcement community, holding the thought that someone with a knife at 21 feet created a deadly force situation. Now, think about that for a moment. This research showed that a knife-wielding person could cover that much ground and use that knife before a person with a gun could draw and fire at the oncoming attacker; add into that scenario the fact that it is more difficult to hit a moving target and the person with a knife does have a chance to carry out a successful attack. This research has been called the Tueller Drill.

In 2012, the television show *Myth Busters* did a similar test to check the results. The results showed that a person with a firearm could draw, shoot, and hit the oncoming attacker at 20 feet. So, it could be argued comfortably that if you are within 19 feet of someone holding a gun and you have a knife, you will be able to attack them successfully with that knife.

So, what does this have to do with a police officer using a knife as a deadly force weapon? There may be a time when the officer has been disarmed or he is unable to get to his firearm and is faced with a deadly force attack. In that case, the first step is to understand the parameters in which a weapon can be used. Knowing that you have 19 feet to work with provides you with a good range to be able to reach your target and effectively deal with the threat.

Typically, when a knife is brought to a police training session, it is to show how an officer can overcome the knife attack. This is also seen in many martial arts studios, as it is usually assumed that the person having the knife is the one on the wrong side of the law, and so, little attention is paid to how to effectively use the knife as an attack weapon. Some would even view this as not being politically correct to teach officers how to stab someone. Yet, if an officer finds that his life is on the line and the only weapon he has is the utility knife on his belt, then he should be aware of how to use it, much like any other tool at his disposal.

Now, there are some things that you need to be prepared for when you use a knife in a deadly force situation. You are now the attacker with the knife. So, in all those self-defense books and videos, you are now taking on the role of the person with the knife. Of course, in this situation, the other person is presenting a life-and-death struggle with you; otherwise, you would not be pulling the knife. Speed, however, is essential. When you use your firearm, speed is with the bullet, so you do not have to be very fast, because the science behind the gun and bullet compensates for distance and time. However, with a knife, in order to be successful in the attack, you must be fast with it. If you have ever observed some of the videos of prison yard shankings, then you will know that these are extremely fast and the hand with the knife does not remain still but constantly moves. In a knife fight, you must utilize speed and aggression, because the knife is a close-up weapon, and this means that you are exposed to all the weapons that your opponent has.

Keeping with that train of thought, remember that the person you are fighting with will use every weapon and means to achieve his goal, which would be to end your life. He will also be very aggressive and up close with you. There is a line in the movie *The Outlaw Josey Wales* that describes this very well. The main character played by actor Clint Eastwood is telling his associates just before a big fight that they have to get mean.

"Now remember, when things look bad and it looks like you're not gonna make it, then you gotta get mean. I mean plumb, mad-dog mean. 'Cause if you lose your head and you give up then you neither live nor win. That's just the way it is."

In a fight for your life, you have to do the same!

Something else you need to be aware of is how messy this is going to be. Some of you who are reading this have been to crime scenes where there has been a lot of blood, and in a knife fight, where you are stabbing someone, you will be creating that scene and possibly one that will be the worst you have ever seen. In a real knife fight, there will be blood, urine, and even feces, as you struggle for your life and this other person for his life. Understand this, because this is reality and not some training hall comment. You are fighting for your life and trying to end someone else's life, because it is a situation where it is either you or them. This will not be clean; it will be messy; be ready for it; and don't be shocked. If you hesitate even for a moment, the outcome may not be to your liking. The knife handle will get slippery and you need to be aware of this to keep your hold on the weapon (Figure 8.1).

With that understanding, we will now move on to how to grip the knife. When it comes to how to hold a knife, some knives are designed to be held in a certain way, just by the design of the handle. Most knives or edged weapons can be used in multiple positions, so just be aware if your knife is one that has a limited design to it. However, the reality is this that you are in the middle of a fight for your life, and how you grab the knife is how you are going to use it. So, just go with whatever you have at the time and use it to the best advantage you can.

Without getting too fancy here, there are basically two grips to familiarize yourself with. One is to grip the knife across the palm, following the line of the extended thumb. The gripping hand then folds naturally around the

Figure 8.1 Knives come in many sizes and shapes. The knife that you carry will often dictate how you will carry it and how you will grip it in an emergency.

handle. The knife is pointed out away from the body in this grip. The second grip is the same, but this time, the blade is pointed toward the body in a reverse grip. Both are demonstrated in Figures 8.2 and 8.3.

The main point about the grip is that it provides you with options as to how to use the knife. For example, a reverse grip will allow you to punch

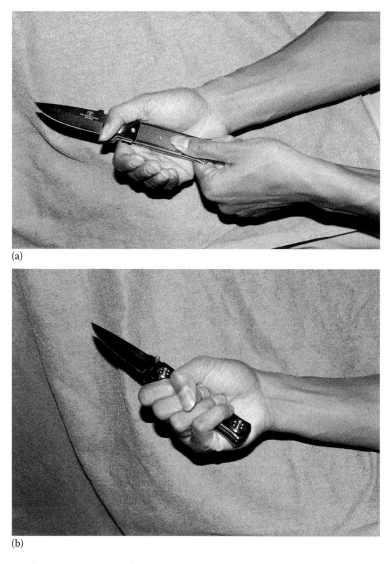

(a)

(b)

Figure 8.2 (a) The forward knife grip holds the knife across the palm, following the line of the extended thumb. (b) The gripping hand folds naturally around the handle. Do not grab the handle with a hammer grip that positions the blade at a 90° angle to the wrist.

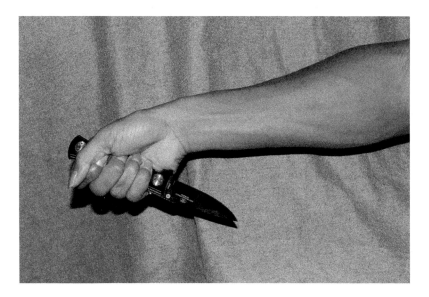

Figure 8.3 The reverse grip is similar to the forward grip, but the blade is held pointing toward the body instead of pointing away.

with the hand and at the same time utilize the blade in a slashing motion. The front grip will not allow you to punch necessarily, but it will give you greater reach and will position the knife well to stab your target.

Not much has actually changed when it comes to using an edged weapon against a human body. When you look for points to attack, there are basically nine directions in which you can move the blade to effect an attack. These come from below as well as above on the target. The following illustration shows the angles and direction of the nine striking points (Figure 8.4).

Basically, the angle of an attack can occur in the following manner:

1. Stab
    a. Upward
    b. Downward
    c. Straight
    d. Diagonal
2. Lateral slash
3. Straight thrust

A side note about targets, trying to get to the primary area of attack, is important, but if the attacker throws up an arm or leg to try to defend the attack, do not try to go around that limb but rather go ahead and attack the limb.

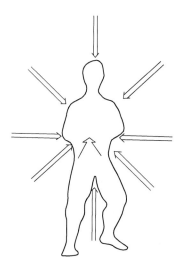

Figure 8.4 This illustration shows the nine directional strikes with an edged weapon.

You are trying to win this encounter, and if the cut disables a limb, the fight can change rapidly and you may then be in a position to utilize more traditional tools. So, always take advantage of what is presented to you in a fight.

Now that you have the basic concepts of how to hold the knife and where you are looking to target it, let's take a look at some attacks that you can use when you are faced with a deadly force situation and you must rely on your knife.

Low-Lying Thrust and Slash

In his video, *Surviving A Street Knife Fight: Realistic Defensive Tactics,* Marc "Animal" MacYoung talked about the most difficult types of attack to defend which is the low-lying thrust and slash. His past years were spent learning about knife fighting while growing up on the streets of Los Angeles; he was a martial artist and even a correctional director. He has been in knife fights and witnessed them, and his opinion may influence you when the time comes and you are utilizing an attack.

The low-lying thrust is difficult to defend, because it comes from below the waist and moves upward. The natural human response is not to look down in a fight but to look directly at your opponent, and so, the attack may not be seen until it is already initiated. In performing this attack, your free hand should come up and across the body of the target to prevent the attacker from being able to strike you and defend against the knife. The hand with the knife then strikes the torso. The reason why you are going after the torso is that the most damage to the body by a knife is in this area. Since you are in a fight for your life, this would be your primary target (Figures 8.5 and 8.6).

Figure 8.5 The knife is in the forward grip and is brought from below the waistline, which makes this a more difficult attack to stop. The opposite hand comes up and delivers an elbow strike or forearm strike but at the very least is pressed against the chest to hamper any kind of defensive move.

Figure 8.6 The knife is brought on target to the midsection of the opponent. By the attack coming from below the waist, it is less likely that the opponent will be able to grab or deflect the knife with his hand or arm.

The low-lying slash is performed in a similar manner, but instead of thrusting the blade into the torso of the target, you slash across the body. The slash attacks several areas of the body, causing damage across the torso area. The attack is not as deep as the thrust, but it does open up more of the body at one time (Figures 8.7 and 8.8).

There may come a time when someone attempts to get your gun and you find that while you have one hand firmly grasped, trying to keep the gun in its holster, you can feel that the struggle is not going well. With your free hand you can grasp your knife so you need it in an available position so you can use this to gain the edge again. This is where a belt knife would come in very handy. The knife is positioned on the gun belt up front, so that it is

Figure 8.7 Performed in the same manner as the low-lying thrust, the low-lying slash has the knife in the reverse grip. The opposite hand again delivers a strike to the upper body of the opponent.

Figure 8.8 The reverse grip means that the knife will be brought across the midsection of the opponent. Do not get your arms crossed as the knife continues its attack but use the opposite arm to then create some distance or to move to another technique.

easily accessible. The free hand can then pull the knife, and it can be used in multiple ways, but the primary focus would be on the hand or hands that are attempting to pull the gun out. By stabbing at the hands, you may gain an edge; however, if this does not work, do not continue but move up the arm and target the more muscular part of the arm. As soon as you feel the grip lighten, of course, pull free and gain a better position to deal with the attack. If you cannot pull free, then understand that this is a fight for your life and use the knife in a more aggressive manner.

Weapon Retention Utilizing a Knife

Many officers carry a knife on their belt, which makes it an ideal backup implement during a struggle over the officer's gun. Remember, if someone is attempting to take your gun, this raises it to a deadly force situation; so, a response with a knife would be appropriate. How you grip the knife will, in all probability, depend on how you reach for it during the struggle. The important point with this use of the knife is to maintain control of your firearm and then deal with the suspect (Figures 8.9 and 8.10).

Figure 8.9 The officer uses the strong hand to secure the firearm in the holster.

Figure 8.10 The officer can draw a knife with the off hand.

In Figures 8.9 and 8.10, as the officer feels the reach for his gun, he clamps his gun side hand on top of the suspect's hand to keep the firearm in the holster. At the same time, he pulls the knife and begins to turn in the direction of the suspect (Figures 8.11 and 8.12).

By attacking the suspect's arm with the knife, the officer is able to pull away, as shown in Figure 8.11, and then move to a more distant position, in order to assess the threat, as shown in Figure 8.12.

Figure 8.11 The knife can then be brought toward the threat while maintaining control of the gun in the holster.

Figure 8.12 The officer can then distance himself from the suspect and resort to the firearm or other tactics depending on the threat.

Body Behind the Blade

During a struggle with a knife, the ability to get your body weight behind your movements enhances the ability to utilize the tool more effectively. The following sequence of photographs demonstrates a struggle involving a knife. The officer is able to lower his center of gravity and get his body behind his arm, as he uses the knife to stop the aggressive action of the suspect (Figures 8.13 through 8.16).

When it comes to edged weapons and police training, the emphasis is usually on how to deal with the threat of such a weapon. Having the ability to use this tool in an effective manner can be the difference of life and death for an officer. Knowing when to use such a weapon, of course, will depend on laws and the general orders of your agency. Developing the skill to use such a tool is something that can stay with you for a lifetime.

Figure 8.13 In this illustration the officer has already pulled a knife to face the threat.

Figure 8.14 The officer centers the body weight and gains a solid footing.

Figure 8.15 The knife is then supported by the arm and body weight of the officer.

Figure 8.16 The knife can then be used against the target.

Special Circumstances 9

Improvise, Adapt and Overcome!

—Tom Highway
Heartbreak Ridge, 1986

You have now seen how the body can aid a person in his or her defense against an attack. Following natural instincts and training can overcome an aggressor. In this chapter, we are going to look at some situations that present unique problems. These are not meant to be total solutions but merely offered as concepts to keep you thinking "outside the box," so to speak. We are often limited by the training and techniques that we receive and do not adapt to situations or look for advantages that may be present if we only see them.

Two-Man Take Down

Officers often respond to complaint calls with a backup. Having two officers present allows for greater safety for not only the officers but also those that they encounter. Faced with a combative or noncompliant subject, officers can work in a coordinated manner and contain and control the subject. The following technique can afford officers the ability to overcome the resistance; this not only reduces the risk of injury to themselves and to the suspect but also shows to an outside observer that the officers use the necessary force to handle the situation and look in complete control.

The two officers must decide in some manner, so that the suspect does not know or understand which officer will go "high" on the subject and which one will go "low." The officer who takes the high position approaches the subject with his weak side and grabs the subject's arm, locking it up to the shoulder, so that the arm is incapacitated. This keeps the subject from being able to grab the high officer's gun and prevents him from being able to fully engage in a fight.

At the same time that the high officer moves, the low officer moves and locks up the subject's legs, preferably just below the knees by using his body weight to then press on the thighs and buckle the knees. The high officer then helps guide the subject's body to the ground, which will keep him in control and, at the same time, will reduce the risk of injury. From this point, the officers can maneuver the prone subject, so that they can perform proper hand-cuffing (Figures 9.1 through 9.4).

Figure 9.1 Two officer take-down tactic.

Figure 9.2 One officer goes "high" and locks the suspect's arm, while moving the officer's head behind the shoulder of the suspect.

This kind of technique, when observed from the outside, appears to be very professional and the officers seem to be completely in control. However, key to this technique is speed. The officers must move in unison, and the subject should not know what is about to happen. If done properly, the subject can be controlled.

Figure 9.3 The second officer goes "low" and takes the suspect's knees.

Figure 9.4 The suspect is taken to the ground.

Improvised Weapons—The Chair

There are times when an officer or an everyday citizen may find himself confronted with someone who has an edged weapon. With the advancement of less lethal force options, such as a taser, an officer can utilize this to diffuse the situation. However, there may be a time when a taser is not available or is not feasible. Going with the force continuum, the officer could go to deadly force against an edged weapon, because it is a deadly tool. But, what about a chair, if one is handy? Have you ever thought about that?

Imagine that you are seeing a chair for the first time. The design makes it a unique defensive weapon in that if held horizontally, there is about a three-foot barrier between the person holding the chair and his or her would-be attacker. Most chairs have four legs that protrude outward. These can be striking points. Then, there is the seat, which acts like a solid barrier between the holder and the person on the other side. The back of the chair can also make for a nice, strong handhold (Figure 9.5).

In short, the chair has many facets that make it a unique tool that can be employed in a variety of situations that an officer may encounter. For example, say an officer was faced with a subject who was acting in a violent manner, perhaps, shouting, clenching his fists, and generally being threatening to those around him. Once the decision has been made to effect an arrest, the chair can act as a barrier in a couple of ways.

Figure 9.5 The chair provides a defense as well as offensive weapon. Notice the four chair legs.

First, just by resting, as it normally does, the chair can be used by an officer as a barrier to keep some distance, until he or she is ready to make the initial move. The suspect will not be able to launch a surprise attack, because the barrier will offer time to the officer, as the suspect will have to go around the barrier to attack. Strange, as it may seem, people will normally try to go around the barrier, even though they can often reach right over it. The visual perception of an object in the way creates in the mind a physical barrier that cannot be penetrated but must be gone around. Even something as simple as a chair can provide enough of a mental distraction to give an officer the extra moment needed to respond to a threat.

If the subject has become violent and the officer feels threatened, then the officer can merely pick the chair up by the backrest and point the four legs at the suspect. This can give the officer several options. He can use the legs to trap the suspect or to pin him against a wall, allowing the backup officer to move in to gain better position, without the suspect being able to move around. If the suspect grabs hold of the chair's legs, then the officer merely releases the chair, moves around, and gains a hold on the suspect. Since the suspect's hands will be busy holding the chair, the officer has time to move and gain control of the suspect before he realizes what is happening.

Another advantage that the chair offers is that it can be used as a take-down device. To execute this maneuver, move the chair into a position where the legs are just past the suspect. Do not do this slowly, as the suspect will not allow you to set up for this. The chair closing in is a threat, and he will attempt some kind of defensive response. So, be prepared to thrust the chair forward. As soon as you have it in position, begin to twist the chair in the direction in which you want to take the subject down. The chair's legs will act as a lever against the suspect's body, and the twisting motion will take him to the ground. Once on the ground, set the chair on top of the suspect, with the legs separating the head from the arms and preferably the arms split. This again creates the visual perception of a barrier and gives the officer an extra moment to gain control of the subject.

However, the usefulness of the chair doesn't stop there. When faced with a combative subject, an officer can use the chair's legs as weapons. By turning the chair so that one of the legs is directly in front of you, you will find two striking points, one high and one low.

A strike to the upper chest by the chair's leg on top will also result in a simultaneous strike to the lower region, possibly the groin of the subject. This will help provide the suspect with sensory overload and again give the officer that extra moment, so that he or she can move in, follow up with control techniques, and effect the arrest.

The chair can be especially effective if the subject has a knife. The very construction of the chair makes it difficult for someone to push a knife through it. The seat is a solid obstacle, and the legs allow the officer distance as well as serve as striking opportunities. Perhaps, the most important item that the chair can provide to an officer in a situation like this is time—time to think of an effective strategy or time to get a better force option and even time to talk the subject out of the weapon. Whatever way you look at it, a simple chair can offer many possibilities as an aid to law enforcement (Figures 9.6 through 9.10).

Figure 9.6 The officer faces a threat from a knife.

Figure 9.7 By using the chair the officer can block any attack from the knife.

Figure 9.8 The officer can use the chair to isolate the suspect's limbs.

Figure 9.9 By twisting the chair the officer can begin to force the suspect to the ground.

In matters of officer survival, the scope of tools available or improvised to resolve the situation shouldn't be limited to the weapons found on the duty belt. There are many items already provided to officers in the types of situations in which they find themselves that can become useful tools. Just as officers are warned of everyday items that can become weapons, such as screwdrivers, forks, and others, they should also be aware of what common items can benefit them. After all, the goal is to do the job as safely as possible and be able to go home after the shift is over.

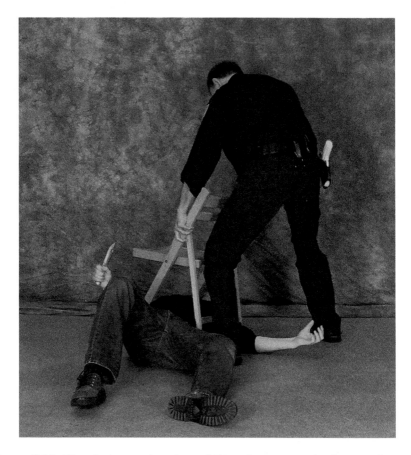

Figure 9.10 The chair can then immobilize the suspect further until control can be gained.

Handgun Retention

One of the most frightening situations that an officer can face is to have someone try and take their firearm. "Officer Killed" statistics show that this fear is warranted, as it is widely known that criminals, both in and outside of prison, routinely practice firearm-disarming techniques.

Under highly stressful situations, such as an attempted disarming, fine motor skills diminish, as the heart rate increases. Documentation on this subject can be found in Bruce Siddle's book, *Sharpening the Warrior's Edge.* He documented the research conducted by Levitt and Gutin on performance and heart rate levels. They discovered that the best responses occurred when the heart rate was between 115 beats per minute and 145 beats per minute. They also showed that when the heart rate is below 115 or over 145 beats per minute, a person's ability to perform diminishes.

This result needs to be taken into account when investing in a handgun retention technique. The best techniques will involve large motor skills, because when you feel that tug on the end of your gun, your heart rate is going to shoot well above 145 beats per minute.

Another concern is response time. It is only logical to believe that if a suspect tries to disarm an officer, he has already mentally rehearsed his actions, and these actions possibly include an attempt to take the officer's life. On the other hand, the officer is not aware of the threat until the actual attempt is made on the gun. This means that the suspect is ahead of the officer with regard to reaction time. The officer must perceive the threat, formulate a plan, and carry out the response. Since all of this takes place in a very short time period, the officer must be able to respond with a technique that will gain back the valuable time lost on recognizing the threat. A handgun retention technique that requires thought, as well as fine motor skills, is not as effective as the one that requires little to no thought and uses large motor skills.

One such technique is the simple spin. The suspect approaches the officer from behind and attempts to grab onto the handle of the weapon and pull it out of the holster. Because of the lost reaction time, the officer needs to respond quickly and efficiently or the gun will be drawn and his life will be in danger. By utilizing a simple turn of his body and using his hand or arm as a lever, the officer can peel the suspect's hand off the firearm. As the turn is completed, the officer's body is between the suspect and the firearm. The non-gun side arm traps the suspect's arm, and by taking a step forward, the officer places pressure on the elbow, creating an armbar, from which follow-up techniques can be used (Figures 9.11 through 9.14).

Figure 9.11 A suspect attempts to take an officer's gun.

Figure 9.12 The officer quickly brings his arm down to the gun, striking the hand with his wrist.

Figure 9.13 The officer then begins to turn toward the suspect, peeling the suspect's hand away from the gun.

Figure 9.14 Notice how the natural body movement aids the officer's technique.

Even if the officer's timing is slightly off and the hand is not peeled away, the turn has trapped the arm and the gun by the officer's body and hand. When the officer steps forward, stretching the suspect out, it enables him to gain control of the firearm easily and puts the suspect at a disadvantage (Figures 9.15 and 9.16).

Figure 9.15 The officer can then stretch out the suspect by pushing on his face and moving the arm into an armbar.

Figure 9.16 The officer can then control the suspect and move them to a hand-cuffing position.

The same technique can be used, no matter which direction the attack comes from. Front attacks, side attacks, and even gun-stripping efforts can be defended by this technique. This type of defense minimizes the officer's time in formulating a plan. As soon as he detects the attempt on the firearm, a quick spin of the body (large muscle groups) and a fast downward arm movement (large muscle groups) can gain back precious time.

Multiple Opponents

There are times when an officer will find that they are facing several people who are intent on causing him harm. The ability of backup to respond in time may not be an option, as the attack could happen before the call for help even goes out. Unlike in television and movies, where an officer will stand in the middle of several opponents, in real life, this could spell disaster.

Much like most seasoned officers will tell a recruit to keep their back to the wall, so that they will not have to worry about what is behind them, so too when facing several opponents. The reality is that, in a fight, your focus becomes very narrowed to the threat that is in front of you. By keeping your back away from the confrontation, you will eliminate one area of attack and can keep your focus on the threat facing you. This may not always be possible, but it is something to keep in mind when considering your options.

When it comes to fighting, we can truly only fight one person at a time. The heroes we see in action movies and television may be able to easily dismantle multiple opponents, but in truth, us mere mortals can only deal with one threat at a time. So, when facing several opponents, you need to realize that you can't fight them all at the same time, so the goal is to face only one at a time. But how do we do that?

The key to this is to move. You cannot stand your ground here. By using tactics from pre-emptive, evasive, and tactical approached, blended together, as the fight changes and the threat changes, you have a better chance of coming out on top. It is more difficult to hit a moving opponent, and so, you should make yourself as mobile as possible to make it as difficult to track and trap you as possible. Move, so that you use the body of the opponent that you are facing to block the path of the other attackers. By doing this constant shifting of your body, you will face only one attack at a time and will be able to move to the next.

If only one of the attackers actually launches his attack, deal with the threat as quickly as you can. If he should fall, leave him in the path of the others to buy you a small advantage and to allow you time to reassess the situation.

When you engage, remember that when you strike, hit with all of your force and move. This is a situation where you cannot remain static, and this cannot be stressed enough. Hit, move, and escape if you can. You can always return when you have backup or do some investigation and gain charges against them.

What you are trying to do is to buy yourself time. By blocking the path of the others and allowing yourself the ability to deal with one threat at a time, you are conserving your energy and focusing on the immediate threat, which is much more manageable for the brain to process than being overwhelmed by several attacks at a time.

The following illustrations will help demonstrate the movement (Figures 9.17 through 9.20).

There is no way to prepare for every situation that you may face in a physical altercation. What you can do is prepare yourself as best as you can by training, exercising, and applying what you have learned. Other things also need to be taken into consideration when facing a physical fight. Understanding the environment that you are in is very important.

Figure 9.17 An officer faces two or more suspects.

Figure 9.18 The officer moves so that he only has to deal with one suspect at a time.

Paying attention to your surroundings, such as being on a gravel road, field, concrete, ice, or mud, could be an aid or a hindrance to your efforts to overcome the attack. Common everyday item can be turned into a weapon if it is readily at hand and if you cannot get to your primary weapons. Just take a moment and look about your house or apartment, and ask yourself: if someone broke in right now, what kind of things could I use to fight with? Even something as simple as a ballpoint pen can be turned into a weapon.

Something to think about in a fight is the flinch reflex. If something is thrown at our eyes, we are going to instinctively respond to this. It is instinct, and so even the best-trained athlete will respond to something coming

Figure 9.19 The officer uses the body of one suspect to block the second.

Figure 9.20 The officer can then deal with the first suspect before engaging the second.

toward his eyes. This will give you a brief moment of time, which you can use to gain an advantage on an attacker. The item tossed can be anything from a ticket book to a briefcase and anything in between. As we hear so often in the business world to "think outside of the box," so too in a real-life fight for your life, all options are on the table.

Knuckle Swipe

There may come a time when you will want to be able to force something out of someone's hand, get them to release a steering wheel, or when they are in a fighting stance, change their focus. One such method to do this is with a hand swipe. This is not meant to be a debilitating blow, but it is a distraction method to gain an edge in a situation.

To perform this technique, you will use your knuckles. The target area is the back of the hand, preferably just behind the knuckles. The move is to reach out and bring your knuckles in a downward motion against the targeted area. This will cause a distraction or possibly force them to open their hand at the least and possibly injure the hand at the most force. The following illustrations demonstrate this (Figures 9.21 and 9.22).

Figure 9.21 When facing an adversary think of the suspect's hands as targets.

Figure 9.22 Strike the back of the suspect's hand with the knuckles.

Elbow Glancing Blow

Another distracting technique is to use the very edge of the elbow and graze the side of the rib cage of your opponent. This is not an elbow strike, but the goal is to just use the tip of the elbow to pull the skin around the bones of the rib cage. This will cause pain, which will distract the opponent from his current course of action and give you the opportunity to gain the advantage either by positioning or using more forceful methods. The following illustrations demonstrate this technique (Figures 9.23 through 9.25).

Figure 9.23 To gain control of a suspect it is sometimes necessary to distract them.

Figure 9.24 By taking the tip of the elbow and grazing the side rib cage the suspect can be temporarily distracted.

Figure 9.25 The officer can then utilize other techniques to gain control.

Grip Release

The ability to escape from a wrist grab is something that everyone should know. It is a basic principle of working against the thumb. A grip can be very powerful, but much like a chain, it is only as strong as its weakest link, and for a hand, that is the thumb. By turning your own wrist so that it is narrow, you work against the thumb and fingers, applying your own force, which frees the hand from the grip. If you find that the grip is too strong, then push into the grip, placing pressure on the back of the thumb and then move to the release. The following photographs show an example of working against the thumb to effect an escape (Figures 9.26 through 9.28).

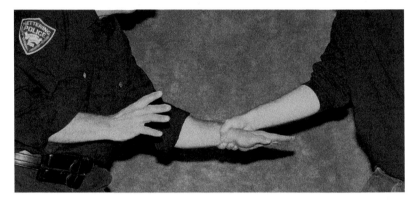

Figure 9.26 Escape from a wrist grab.

Figure 9.27 Straighten the fingers on the hand and begin to exert pressure against the thumb.

Figure 9.28 Bending the elbow and pulling away from the thumb and finger, the wrist grab will be broken.

There will always be circumstances that will appear during encounters with people that cannot be covered in every book or training video. Make use of whichever opportunities and targets are presented to you to gain the advantage. You must, of course, balance this with the situation you are in, the amount of force you are authorized to apply, and any general orders by your agency. The key is to adapt your training to the situation and use force in an appropriate manner.

Integrated Use-of-Force Training 10

A martial artist who drills exclusively to a set pattern of combat is losing his freedom. He is actually becoming a slave to a choice pattern and feels that the pattern is the real thing. It leads to stagnation because the way of combat is never based on personal choice and fancies, but constantly changes from moment to moment, and the disappointed combatant will soon find out that his "choice routine" lacks pliability. There must be a "being" instead of a "doing" in training. One must be free. Instead of complexity of form, there should be simplicity of expression.

—Bruce Lee
Bruce Lee Jeet Kune Do, 1997

When it comes to preparing an officer for a situation where they may have to use force, training in the academy and in the various methods of force is effective only to a point. The issue of an officer's comfort zone with a physical encounter should also be addressed. When dealing with an officer's survival, being able to apply the techniques in a classroom setting is one step; by adding some of the tactics discussed in this book, officers will have the opportunity to apply their training more effectively—but there is the issue of a comfort zone.

One of the reasons why seasoned warriors always performed better in battle is because they had been there and done that before. They had earned their way by surviving other situations similar to the current one that they are facing, and so, their reaction time to the incident is quicker, because they have observed the behavior before, felt the things that they are feeling now before, and have raised their comfort level with this kind of experience more so than their counterpart who is experiencing it for the first time.

This works in the sports world also. When you think of teams that go to the championship games, often it is the one with seasoned veterans guiding the young rookies or the first-time-to-the-big-show members of the team that win the game. The scenario is same with veteran police officers, as opposed to recruits. The veterans are more comfortable and more aware of what is taking place, because their comfort level is much higher, and they are able to observe more than the recruits who are seeing this for the first time and finding that their senses are a bit overwhelmed because they are out of their comfort zone.

The question then becomes: how to provide the experience of a violent encounter to officers, so that their comfort level is raised, yet to do it in a safe environment, where mistakes can be corrected and the officers can grow from the experience? This type of training would be able to add to the officers' confidence, so that when they do face an encounter on the street, they will be more prepared and better able to respond in an effective manner. The answer is an integrated use-of-force training program.

At a police instructor's training seminar, defensive tactics expert Tony Blauer explained the issue of the comfort zone like this. "It is not the danger that makes us afraid, it is the fear of the danger." Even going with the words of Franklin D. Roosevelt, "The only thing we need to fear is fear itself," shows that we can be our own worst enemy during a time of crisis.

When you think of a comfort zone, think of it like a circle that surrounds you. This is where you are most at ease with dealing with situations. As you move beyond that zone and start doing things that you may be familiar with but not necessarily practiced in, you will enter the discomfort zone. Here, you can operate, but you will need time to process the situation and to evaluate responses. Once you move beyond the discomfort zone, you have entered the "oh crap" zone or basically in totally unfamiliar territory. Here, you are totally out of your element and are working off of your basic instincts. The idea then is to raise that comfort circle as large as you can, so that you do not enter the last circle (Figure 10.1).

The test of any police training is its effectiveness on the street. If there is a flaw in the training, there is no way to correct it until after the situation is resolved. That could have disastrous consequences for the officer, the department, and the citizens they serve.

Realistic integrated use-of-force training was created with the goal of reaching beyond the standard training methods and place officers in a realistic setting in which everything is present, just as it could happen on the street. Not only do the officers have to deal with possible suspects, but they also have to control their emotional response.

During a violent street encounter, as in the training sessions, an officer's motor skills diminish, as the "fight or flight" syndrome takes over. Small muscle movements become hampered, and large motor skills are what remain. Unless a fancy technique has been practiced many times over in a physical attack, the officers will become ineffective because they rely on small motor movements rather than the large ones. This is why the military and martial artists practice their training over and over, so that the skill will be there when required. Using integrated use-of-force training will provide an appreciation for the officers for their ability to perform under these conditions and will allow them to expand their comfort zone.

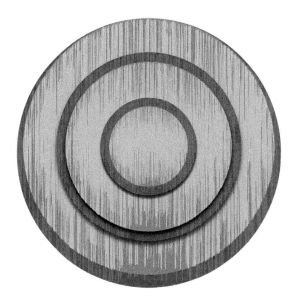

Figure 10.1 Our comfort zone is where we like to, but to grow and develop, we need to increase the size of the comfort zone and reduce the other zones, thereby becoming more comfortable in rapidly evolving situations. The inner circle is the comfort zone, and as you move to the outer circles, we are less comfortable and have less confidence in dealing with the situation. (Courtesy of pixabay.com.)

Law enforcement training methods have not changed much since the 1970s. Recruits go through basic training, which includes firearms and force options. Ongoing training is usually dissected and dealt with on an individual basis. When it is time to perform firearm qualifications, officers go to the range: defensive tactics are taught in the gym, and each force option has its own rules and gurus, but merging of these force choices, as you would experience on the street, does not usually take place. Yet, no officer who finds himself in a violent attack will rely on one form of force. The situation changes quickly, and force options need to be integrated, but unless it is practiced to move from one form of force to another, say a baton to a gun, the officer could lose valuable seconds and possibly even lose the fight.

This training methodology has worked, up to a point, but it falls short of the expectations of court decisions and officers themselves. These prior training philosophies were often static, keeping the officers detached from the emotional response experienced on the street in a real situation. Such training has kept officers thinking of using one type of force option at a time, instead of being able to incorporate all measures of force into one total training system.

Certainly, today, the technology is available to an all-inclusive style of training. With the advent of some innovative training aids, officers can be provided with a training situation that would allow them to encounter a scene where it could escalate from verbal force to deadly, depending on the performance of the officer. This can be done in a safe training environment and will add realism to their training, which, in turn, will give them the experience that they need to increase their comfort zone on the street.

However, before the training can take place, there are some things that need to be in place to ensure that the training environment will be realistic, yet safe for both the officer and the role player that he will be facing. The goal, of course, is not only to prepare an officer to the highest level with his training in various use-of-force options and their techniques but also to prepare the total officer in the best possible manner.

First, of course, it is recommended that officers receive academy or in-service training in firearms, defensive tactics, taser, and OC spray, as well as receive some verbal de-escalation training before attempting this kind of enhanced training. A good foundation should be in place before the training can be taken to the next level, and a more realistic training experience should be created. With this kind of foundation the officer will be able to draw upon all of their options and apply them just like they would on the street in a real encounter.

If an agency is going to place this style of training on, then the next step to add realism would be a recommendation to review the department's use-of-force reports and look for those situations most common to an officer where force was needed. This may change from jurisdiction to jurisdiction because of the citizens and type of crime in that area. However, if this training is being conducted by officers or others on their own, then a good starting place would be the five typical situations that LA officers found themselves in, as mentioned in Chapter 1. This again is to be as realistic as possible, so staying with actual encounters will accomplish this.

Once the scenarios are decided upon, the next most important thing is to obtain the equipment that will be needed in order to conduct the training. This is where the technology today has greatly enhanced the ability to conduct this kind of training.

Training gear such as fully padded suits are readily available in the market today. These suits provide protection to a role player from head to foot and allow officers to go hands on in an aggressive way to test their skills, yet keep all involved safe. Many different companies make these suits today, and this is vital to have in order to perform physical encounters.

Simulated weapons, such as knives and guns, are also good to have on hand. These again will add to the realism of what the officer is about to experience. However, just as important are training aids such as batons, tasers, and inert OC spray, if an officer has these available when they are working on the street. This will permit them to use these devices just as they would do on the street, or they may have to transition from one force option to another and deal with securing the item in order to use the next one. This issue alone is often lacking in most static style training.

Another innovation in technology today is the creation of simulated ammunition, so that officers can use their own weapon during a training scenario, so they will experience an incident by using the equipment that they have on hand. There are many different versions of this. Some companies offer a simulated bullet that fires with a cartridge, just as if it were a live round to others, where the chamber of the gun is blocked, but the gun cycles just like if it were firing live rounds. This option, of having the gun cycle, run dry of ammunition, again provides the ability to confront officers with a situation where their immediate resources may be overwhelmed and they have to use additional magazines, weapons, and skills to survive the encounter.

Additional items to obtain would be the usual for this kind of training, such as helmets, face shields, gloves, and other items, to provide protection, so that the risk of injury is reduced. As with any kind of physical training, there is the risk of bumps and bruises.

Once the training scenarios have been selected and the equipment purchased, the true key to this kind of training needs to be gathered. The key to a successful training session rests with the role players who will engage the officer. This is critical because they must present the scenario in as realistic manner as possible, so the officer will gain the full benefit from the experience. In order to do this, the role players must be familiar with the training equipment, training goals, and tactics and techniques of the officer.

Each scenario should be designed in a way so that the role player knows what outcome is ideal for the officer in the situation. Part of the key to success here is that the role players must understand that, at the end of the scenario, they must lose. This is a very important point! In order to develop confidence in the officers, they need to be pushed to a higher comfort zone but not pushed beyond their capability. In this manner, the officers will have to reach down deep inside themselves to overcome the scenario but will win, and by doing so, they will understand that they have accomplished this on their own. As time goes by, the officers will gain confidence and experience, and the scenarios can be pushed further, depending on their abilities.

Another item to keep in mind is that role players have a tendency to get tired or bored with performing the same scenario over and over again if you have multiple officers attending the training. They might need to be rotated to a different scenario to keep them fresh, but a reminder of the goal of the scenario and their part will help keep them on track and focused on the officers in the training, which is the purpose of the training.

In order to accomplish this, a role player will need to place his ego on hold. Everyone wants to win and everyone likes to get the edge on someone, but here, in this training, the officer is the one who wins and the role player needs to remember this. Egos can also make the situation more difficult, so that it becomes a no-win scenario, and this defeats the purpose of the training.

This presents the next part of the training in that there needs to be a safety monitor for each scenario. Just like the role player, the safety monitor ensures that the training is realistic but safe. The safety monitor also keeps the end result in mind and keeps the scenario on track for the training objective.

The safety officer performs several very important functions. First and foremost, he must ensure that no live ammunition is present and only the training weapons are present in the training scenario. The officers and role players need to be checked for anything that is a weapon as well. Often, people will have a knife or other item on them; these items should be removed from the training section, so that there are no items present that can actually be called a weapon. This would also extend to anyone who may be observing the training, as there is no room for error when this kind of training is taking place.

If this training is taking place near residences or within a jurisdiction, then proper notifications should be made. Law enforcement and residents should be aware of the training, so that they will not be alarmed. The simulated ammunition sounds just like its real counterpart and may draw concerns from those around. So, this should be done before conducting the training.

Then, the safety officer will monitor the scenario, and it is recommended that he have a whistle or other device to signal a stop in action. While monitoring the scenario, the safety officer watches for the safety of the role players as well as that of the officer. The safety officer also needs to be aware if the scenario is going too far off course, and if so, he should stop the action and discuss how to proceed from that point on. Ultimately, the safety officer is the one that terminates each scenario. When he is satisfied that the training objective has been met, a signal, usually a whistle, will signal the stoppage of action, and then, a debriefing can occur.

To begin the training, the safety officers should hold a training briefing with all involved. Here, safety guidelines and the equipment should be explained. Everyone should be familiar with the safety equipment and how to use it. This would also be a good time for the safety officers to do their weapons check to ensure that no live weapons are present.

If liability forms are to be signed for the training, this should be completed at this time. The first-aid station should be identified in case of an injury so that all will know where to go for assistance.

The purpose of the training and the expectation from the officer in the performance should be explained. This will alleviate some of the apprehensiveness that may develop in some officers before the training takes place. The safety protocols need to be explained clearly, so that everyone will know when to stop the action—for example, when they hear the whistle, they should freeze where they are.

Once this is completed, the training can take place. The officers will face a situation as close to a realistic situation as possible, with the safety of their own training. Once the scenario is completed, then the officers and safety officer can discuss their performance during the scenario to help debrief them and to point out things that they did well and those areas that they may need to improve upon. This is important because officers may view their actions in one way but observers may notice something else.

If possible, the scenario should be videotaped, so that during the reviewing process, the officers can watch their performance, which also helps them understand items that they may have missed or things that they may have improved upon. This observation part of the training can be just as enlightening as the training itself.

When the training is completed, officers will have a very real sense of their abilities. They will have been able to combine force options, just as they would on the street, and also deal with suspects who are bent on taking the fight to them. Here, the training and tactics that they have learned in class and in the classroom can come to life in an environment where they can test their skills safely.

This story told by Lt. Col. David Grossman in his *Bullet Proof Mind* training to help illustrate the importance of training like this will perhaps express the concept even better.

To insulate the point of how simulating stressful or fearful encounters can inoculate against the destroyer of extreme fear response in combat, Grossman told the story of deputy sheriff Jennifer Fulford. When she surprised three home invaders in a garage, she took incoming fire from all three, and was shot 10 times (the bad guys were hitting her with about one in every four shots). All the time, however, she was returning fire, and hitting with every shot. She killed one, lost use of her strong hand, did a left-handed, one-handed reload, killed a second one, and the third ran away. Today she has recovered and back on the beat. Fulford said 'I am the product of my training,' and went on to say that the whole incident was less stressful than her simulation training.

Chad D. Baus
Buckeye Firearms Association, 2008

Report Writing— Courtroom Testimony

11

This report, by its very length, defends itself against the risk of being read.

—Winston Churchill
The Winston Churchill Handbook: Everything You Need to Know About Winston Churchill, 2016

The ill and unfit choice of words wonderfully obstructs the understanding.

—Francis Bacon
Novum Organum, 1620

Report Writing

There are more than just physical techniques that keep an officer safe, when it comes to use-of-force situations. The officer being able to deal with the aggression on the street is one thing, but there is the situation of the court-room and possible charges of police abuse and brutality that officers must realize each time they use force. This is why it is extremely important that officers exercise their writing techniques and improve their report writing, so that the documentation that they present in a report provides a clear picture of what they saw and explains why they reacted as they did. Officers are very good at observing behavior and at being able to respond to it, but they are not always adequate at relating that information so that there is no doubt, as to why they used the force that they did.

There are courses, books, videos, and other resources that can be used to enhance an officer's ability to communicate what happened during an event. The in-dash videos are of help if they catch the events in the frame of the camera, as well as the microphones are helpful if they catch what is said. Many departments have issued to officers body cameras, which again pro-vide information on what happened and could be shown in court, but an officer will still write a report. What is offered here are some tips in general for officers to consider when writing their report. This is meant only to serve as a guideline to be considered and to give the reader material to focus on when it comes to writing a report. Each police department will have its own guidelines and expectations on use-of-force reports, and those should be followed as well.

There was a U.S. Supreme Court case that did set some standards for use of force, and this should be articulated in the police report. The case of *Graham v. Connor, 490 U.S. 386 (1989)*, set a standard to be *objective reasonableness*. This would be the issue that courts would review when it came to the issue of use-of-force. So, what is objective reasonableness? It can be articulated in several ways.

The court set down some applications of objective reasonableness that they would use to determine if the force used was appropriate or not. The first of these is the *totality of the circumstances*. Police force encounters are not static incidents but rather encompass many issues and items. There could be other events or issues that were occurring at the same time, and all of these must be considered when deciding the totality of the event. Force is not found in a vacuum but rather as a result of multiple factors, involving the officer, suspect, surroundings, witnesses, and other things that could have had an influencing effect.

Another area that will help determine objective reasonableness would be this concept of what the perspective of a reasonable officer is. Would another officer make the same decision in the same situation, given all of the details of the incident? Officers are humans and are influenced by their very nature, and so, some may overreact and some may underreact, but the question would be applied to the actions of the officer if they were what a reasonable officer in a similar situation would do? This standard is something that you see whenever there is a high-profile case and news shows bring on experts to discuss the events, and they will state what is reasonable for the given facts, as they know them.

When the force was actually applied will also help in determining the objective reasonableness. Was the force applied at the appropriate time or was it after the suspect had become compliant or no longer resisting? This will be examined again with the perspective of what a reasonable officer would do. It is clear that if a suspect lashes out at the officer, and in response to the attack, the officer uses force, then this is a non-issue. However, when the officer becomes the aggressor, whether it is to effect an arrest or to stop aggressive behavior, the point that the force is applied becomes a very important point—one that should be spelled out in the police report to explain why force was needed and applied.

The High Court recognized that police and citizen encounters are very fluid, and because of this, they understand that these situations can be very intense and evolve very rapidly. Therefore, the report must show the changes in a chronological order, so that someone reviewing the events can have a clear picture of how quickly things changed, which caused the officer to take the action that he did. By articulating these events, the reasonable officer standard can be met much more clearly.

In order to fulfill the requirements under Graham, the court decided on four key factors that should be yardsticks used to determine proper use of force. The first of these is the severity of the crime involved. Crimes are given penalties and labels such as felony and misdemeanor, because the rules of society that were violated are based on the impact on society, and responses to them would be different. The next issue would be whether or not the suspect posed an immediate threat to the officer or to others. Along with the immediate threat, if the suspect was actively resisting arrest is also an issue that the courts want to know. The last point the court made was that they wanted to know if the suspect was attempting to flee and in what manner was he doing this.

If your report covers these items and the force was within department guidelines and something that a reasonable officer would do, then the force utilized will not be a problem. However, the officer involved in the use of force must articulate these things in the report. If they are not in the report and if the officers find themselves in court explaining their actions, they will then need to explain why they did not include this information in the report, and this can cause a whole new set of problems.

Let us look at how a report could go, approaching it from a chronological order. This approach can also help remember the events as you begin to write the report.

If we follow the force continuum, then the first level of force is the actual police presence. Just by being there, the officer presents the force of the uniform and the authority that society has placed on them. So, when writing a report, it should explain why the officer was there in the first place—for example, dispatched, observed by routine patrol, and directed by a citizen. How the officer arrived should also be included, for example, in a marked police vehicle in uniform and unmarked police vehicle in plain clothes. This kind of detail will help focus your thoughts as you begin to write the report and will also establish the authority and reason for being there. An example could be that the officer dispatched on a call of domestic dispute and arrived in a marked vehicle at this address.

The next part of the report should be more detailed, because here you are beginning to explain your observations of the scene on your arrival. This helps establish what you observed as you approached. Were there indications of an altercation or violence? Were there items that you noted that concerned you for any reason? What perceptions did you have as you approached? How many suspects were present and how many officers were there? All of this helps show the reader and ultimately the court the view of the scene through your eyes.

What did you say on your approach should also be considered, especially if you issued any commands to any of the people you encounter. This again falls along with the force continuum, because verbal commands are next up from officer's presence. This also establishes the mindset that you had at the time you encountered the scene, but just as important is the response that you received from the subjects present.

Your observations on a subject's verbal and nonverbal actions should be noted in the report. Take note of their attitude as well as their appearance. These may seem like small details, but they again put in place the foundation for why you took the steps that you did to handle the situation. Recall Chapter 1 and some of the nonverbal cues that someone exhibits before a fight; note any of these and any others actions that are noteworthy. What you are doing here is painting a picture of what you observed and how the people responded to your presence—do this even if the event was video- and audiotaped.

As you continue to describe the incident, develop the report with the important points—who-what-where-when-how-why frame of mind. This will help focus your mind on the events and recall the details that led to the encounter and the responses from you as well as from the others involved.

Include again any conversation that you had with the subjects, especially if you have issued any kinds or commands to them. Also, note what their reaction was. This shows how the situation evolved into the eventual confrontation and the steps that were taken to handle the situation before it escalated to a physical encounter. Important points to bring up are the age, size, and physical condition of not only the suspect but also the officer. If the suspect is, say, a professional boxer, then his capability to inflict injury on an officer would be greater than that of a typical college student. Previous knowledge of a suspect can also be important, for example, if the suspect had prior military training or had mental illness, which were known at the time of the encounter. Is there alcohol or drug use suspected at the time of the encounter, and are there weapons in the area that could be used by a suspect?

Then, describe the encounter. How did the suspect attack you? What was your response? Here is where you want to be as accurate in your description of the techniques you applied as you can be. Each defensive tactics system has a nomenclature of the techniques that are taught; use those terms when describing what you did and how you applied the force on the subject. By using this nomenclature, you eliminate the possibility of misinterpretation of what you did and how you did it. This will help defend you, should the case be presented in court. One thing defense attorneys will look for is whether there are inconsistencies in your report and whether there is room for interpretation on what you did. The key is to be specific and to use terminology from the training that you have received.

Once you have gained control of the subject, describe any control techniques or tactics that you used to maintain control until handcuffing had taken place. When describing the handcuffing in your report, be sure to mention that you checked each one to ensure that they were not on too tight and that they were double locked (keeps them from creeping tighter).

If you did anything further to de-escalate the situation, you should mention this. Did you try to talk to the subject to calm him down? Perhaps, you explained why you did the action that you needed to do or anything else that may be important to show how the situation was handled and diffused. Remember that you are painting a picture here to show how your efforts were necessary and brought on by the actions of the suspect.

However, reporting does not stop there. When the subject is being transported, often this can also be of importance to a case, when it comes to testify in court. Notice the suspect's demeanor while in the transporting vehicle and any utterances they may make. Include if they continued to struggle or attempted any other physical violence while in the transport and also any verbal abuse that was issued.

If the subject is injured, be sure to get him the necessary medical assistance and note this in your report as well. If the suspect is claiming an injury, it is a good idea to have this photographed, even if there are no visible signs of injury. The photograph will help establish this and will also help show what you observed during the encounter.

This will also apply if the officer sustained any injury. It is just good practice to document and photograph injuries, as the court may want to see them, and it helps establish the violence of the encounter with the suspect. So, mentioning the medical facility that offered treatment is also noteworthy for the report.

Items that should be included in the report could be witness statements from others who were present but did not participate in the situation; this could be from bystanders and fellow officers as well. This will provide additional views of the events that led to the use of force and the force used to control the situation. Gathering any evidence and noting it in the report should also be completed.

Some key points to keep in mind is, again, that this is not meant to be all-inclusive information on report writing and that each police agency may have different requirements and format for their reports. This is presented to guide an officer, so that he has these items in his mind while he is going through the event and recording it.

Keep the report simple. This may sound confusing when you look at all the information that should go into a report. However, keeping it simple, just to the facts of the incident, helps focus the report and provides the reader with a clear impression of what took place.

Keeping the reader in mind when you write is also very important. The readers only knows what is placed before them on the page. There may be details that you take for granted or figure that everyone knows, but in reality, the reader may not know it. Cover all of the events as if you are telling someone who is not in law enforcement. Do this from the frame of mind that they have no knowledge of the incident and are hearing the facts for the first time. This is very true, as prosecutors, defense attorneys, and judges will read the report but were not on the scene, so they need to have a clear picture of the events.

Write the report to express to the reader what took place and not to impress. Do not embellish or interpret things that happened. Merely do what it says—report. Give a clear, concise accounting of the events that took place. Keep this thought in mind that any report you create could and can end up in the hands of the nine justices who sit on the Supreme Court—what do you want them to think of your report? Keep to the facts and be sure to articulate your reasoning for your actions, so that someone not associated with law enforcement can easily understand the report.

You did a good job on the street and handled a stressful situation—take the time you need to prepare a report worthy of the effort that you put in on the street.

Being an Effective Witness

The ability to write a good report that documents the incident well is but one more step in the process of the courts and their review of a use-of-force incident. The courtroom is another step along the way, and it is also one that officers need to be aware of, so that they can offer the court a clear report of what took place. To do this, there are some things that you should think about before taking the oath and sitting down to be questioned.

One of the reasons why you write the report as detailed as talked about in the previous section is that, when your time to testify arrives, it will be much later than when you wrote that report. Memories of events do fade, and the report is there to refresh you on the events as they happened. Because of this, it is wise to take the time to review your report before you take the witness stand. You can be sure that the defense attorney has gone through your report with a fine toothed comb, and while the prosecutor has read it, he may be relying on you to recall the event in detail. So, you need to take it on yourself to review your report.

Now, it is obvious that no report will have every detail. With the use of cameras now, more of the event will be captured, but this is from the single viewpoint of the camera lens. Your testimony will be from what you observed and what you did. Although your report may not include everything that took place, you should have included the most important details. When you testify, be careful about testifying about things that you did not mention in the report. While this may be true and you may have not included it in your report, it can also look like you are changing the events now to suit your own needs. This is why that report is so very important—if you leave out key information and try to present it on the stand, it may not be allowed by the court if it is news to the defense. They do have the right of discovery, and if you are offering new information, it must be given to them before you take the stand.

Once you have reviewed your report, try to meet with the prosecutor before going into the court. Not all prosecutors offer this, so it is a good idea on your part to seek them out and get them to sit down with you. Remember, you are the one that will be on the witness stand, not the prosecutor. It is always good to be as prepared as you can, so do not take this lightly, especially in a use-of-force case.

When you meet with the prosecutor, ask him to go over what he thinks of the case and the evidence. Ask him what questions he is going to ask you while you are on the stand. This offers you the opportunity and if you think that there is something important that he is not asking about, you can bring this up. Here again, by you being prepared, you can assist the prosecutor in being prepared. The next part is very important, ask the prosecutor what kind of questions you can expect on cross-examination. By gaining insight into weaknesses in your report and areas that a defense attorney will try to question you on can help shore up your testimony. A prosecutor should be able to look at the case from both sides of the courtroom and should be able to have an idea of where the defense is going to go. Here is the time to discuss with the prosecutor that if there is information lacking in your report but vital to the case, how to get this into the court testimony. The main issue here is presenting the case facts to the court, so that everyone in the courtroom has a clear view of what you encountered when you did apply force and all that happened during the application of the force.

This is about as much preparation as you can do before going to court, but it is worth every minute you spend on it. There is no way to review things once you are on the stand, and your memory needs to be fully refreshed as if the incident occurred the night before.

Just by the fact that you are an officer, you are given credibility in the court. This is why, it is so very important that an officer never lies when giving testimony. One lie or one little fabrication will destroy your credibility in court forever. You will basically never be given the benefit of the doubt again, so this is very important—only tell the truth. No case or no arrest is worth tainting your honor and your career.

Even without telling a lie though, there are things that you can do, which can diminish your credibility with a jury and a judge. Juries look for certain things in witnesses to assess whether or not they are providing truthful and factual information. Just like when you are talking to co-workers and they are telling a story, you are assessing their story based on what you observe and what you hear. So, juries will be looking at your attitude and appearance on the stand. Appearances give us our first impression of someone, and once that is established, it is very difficult to change it. So, be professional not only in appearance but also in your demeanor.

Juries will also be listening to how you testify and your memory of the events. Again, this is why it is so important to review that report. If a jury sees that you are trying to think of things when relating the events, your memory of those events may come into question. However, if you are prepared and able to recount the events in a clear and concise manner, then your credibility will remain with them.

If you display a bias or an interest in how the case turns out can also diminish your credibility in court. Just as with anyone we meet, if they have a bias in a situation, then we begin to take their statements with a grain of salt, because they are not objective. As a police officer, you are supposed to be objective and have no personal stake in the outcome. If you show this bias, then, of course, other comments that you make will not carry as much weight with the jury.

There are two very important things to keep in mind as an officer during your testimony. Do not overstate facts to make you or your case look better, and do not suppress facts that could be favorable to the defendant. If you do either of these, it will show that you have an interest and bias in the case, and much of what you testified to will be viewed with suspicion on the part of the court. Your testimony should be impartial, clear, concise, and, most importantly, factual. If you stay that course, then you will be viewed as credible, and your testimony will carry a lot of weight with a jury.

Keeping all that in mind, you are ready to take the stand. Now, this can be a bit of an intimidating process if you have not testified before, or, even if you had a few times, it can still create a bit of anxiety, and you may be nervous. Some indicators of someone who is nervous on the witness stand can be such things as his or her voice is softer or lower than normal or he or she mumbles words. Slumping in the witness chair is another, and just think for a moment how that looks to a jury if an officer in the court is slumping while seated. Speaking too rapidly is also a cue, and this can also make you difficult to understand, much like talking too softly. Forgetting simple things like names can also be an indicator of being nervous.

Now, the good news is that we are all nervous at some point when we take the witness stand. This is normal. So, to help combat this nervousness, make yourself sit straight in the chair but not like a stiff board. Imagine that you are sitting in a classroom and the chief shows up. You would be sitting straight in your chair then; so, do the same in the court. The next thing is to remember to breathe. This may seem simple, but it is very important, because when we are nervous, we tend to hold our breath, and because of that, we are taking in less oxygen, which can have an effect on the body. Holding your breath or breathing very shallow will actually only add to your nervousness. So, take the time to take a few breaths to help slow you down and calm you down.

When you are asked a question by the prosecution or defense, listen to the question carefully, so that you fully understand the question. This is not a race, so there is no reason to fire rapid responses back. Think before you speak. Yes, you have heard this all your life, but in court, it is very important. You must engage your brain before your mouth. This is why it is so important to understand the question being asked, so that you answer it in a clear manner.

If you are nervous and notice the signs, be aware, and when you talk in court, speak louder and slower than you feel is necessary. When we are nervous, we do have the tendency to speak rapidly, but we may be unaware of it ourselves. Just think back about when you were in school and needed to give a 10-minute speech. You practiced it at home and had it down to 10 minutes on the second; only when you gave the presentation in class, you were 2 minutes short of the mark. That is because of the rapid speech that we do when nervous. Slow and steady, plain and clear, is how you want to speak while on the stand.

Eye contact is also very important. When someone is speaking to you, look him or her in the eye. This is not only the polite thing to do, but it also adds to your image for the jury of being professional. Just imagine your impression of someone who is on the stand but never looked at the person speaking to him—how credible would you think he was?

If you do not understand the question, do not be shy about asking the person to rephrase it, so that you fully understand it. Do not answer a question that you are not sure about. So, try to gain a full understanding of what you are being questioned on, so that you offer only that information. Again, when it comes to credibility, think about how credible you would think someone was if you clearly heard the question and the person answered something completely different, not addressing the question.

When it comes to answering questions, there is a difference between the phrases I don't know and I don't understand. If you answer "I don't know," it means you were not aware of that information or that event. It could be that you didn't see it or were not looking in that direction. However, if you say that you do not remember, this is when you are not sure you did or did not see this but cannot recall the information at this time. You may have merely forgotten it, and it could come to you later. For example, let's say, you are at the mall and you run into someone you know but cannot recall their name. Now, you do know them, so you know the information, but while you are talking to them, you cannot remember their name. Then, several minutes after they have left, the name comes to you very clearly, because you have now recalled it. So, when you say "I don't remember," it does leave the door open for you to recall it later, but if you say "I don't know," then the door is shut on that information.

During the course of your testimony, you may want to refer to your report. This is permissible, but try not to make it a habit. Before you look at it, ask for permission of the judge to do so, and it would be good to identify the part that you would want to refer to in order to refresh your memory. If you have a notebook that you use, and that is what you want to refer to, remember that defense must have access to this, and it also means that it is open to the court. So, if you have other things in that notebook, like personal items, this can now come out in court. So, keep notebooks professional, and if you do refer to them, ask first.

When it comes to providing testimony in court, understand that your role as an officer of the court is to give testimony to the facts of the event. In the case of a use-of-force incident, you must explain to the court why the force was necessary. So, articulate the behaviors and actions of the accused that led you to take the action that you did. Be clear with what you did, and if you applied defensive tactics, explain the tactic by name. This again explains why that report is so very important.

There are five golden rules when it comes to being an effective witness, according to attorney and police trainer, Valerie VanBrocklin, who offered these tips to officers at a police trainer's conference. As long as you follow these five rules, your testimony will be viewed as being an officer of the court, presenting facts to be evaluated; those rules are as follows:

1. Honesty
2. Brevity
3. Clarity
4. Fairness
5. Self-control

Follow these rules and you will find the experience of testifying in court to go well. The main thing is to present a clear picture to the court of the events that took place and what you saw, observed, and then acted upon, so that any force you apply will be fully understood by the court.

Effective Witness Checklist

1. Review your police report
2. Meet with the prosecutor and discuss:
    a. Your testimony
    b. Prosecution questions
    c. Defense attorney questions
    d. Errors or omissions in your report
    e. Evidence
3. Be aware that you may be nervous, and take steps to minimize it
4. When you testify, remember:
    a. Listen before you speak
    b. Answer only the question being asked of you
    c. Speak louder and slower
    d. Speak clearly and concisely
    e. Keep eye contact with whoever speaks to you
    f. Ask to rephrase any question that you do not fully understand
    g. Use "I don't know" and "I don't remember" in proper places
    h. Refer to your report only as needed and ask if you can do this
    i. Describe the events do not offer a conclusion or opinion unless asked
5. Practice the five golden rules
    a. Honesty
    b. Brevity
    c. Clarity
    d. Fairness
    e. Self-control

Court Decisions 12

The President and the Congress are all very well in their way. They can say what they think they think but it rests with the Supreme Court to decide what they have really thought.

—Theodore Roosevelt
Theodore Roosevelt Quotes & Facts, 2016

Presidents come and go, but the Supreme Court goes on forever.

—William Howard Taft
The Life and Times of William Howard Taft, 1998

In the United States, the legislative branch creates laws that the executive branch will execute, but the judicial branch can modify or eliminate the laws completely. Anyone in law enforcement knows how a law can be changed by a single ruling from the High Court. Perhaps, no better example can be found than *Miranda v. Arizona*. Before the ruling in that case, officers did not have to advise anyone that they had the right to remain silent or that they could have an attorney present with them if they were being interrogated. The mindset before that ruling was that it was each individual's responsibility to know what his or her rights were. However, with that ruling, the court changed how interrogations were conducted, and if the rules were not followed, evidence obtained during such an interrogation would not be allowed in a court hearing.

When it comes to the issue of force and the police, the High Court has not remained silent. The basic premise that police agencies work under is the thought that they are allowed to use the force necessary to stop aggressive behavior and to effect arrests. While the premise is sound, the High Court has placed limits on that ability to apply force and, in some cases, has enhanced an officer's ability to use force. In today's climate, however, an officer needs to be aware of what rulings are in play, as unlike *Miranda v. Arizona*, no one will advise him during the use-of-force incident what force is allowed at that moment in time. It is up to the officer to know his rights and limits when it comes to the application of force.

While this is not meant to be a comprehensive look at all the cases that apply to the use of force by law enforcement, we will take a look at some that officers should be familiar with. You should be aware of your own local and state laws, as well as the general orders of your organization. These are perhaps the best guidelines for you to follow, as general orders are usually updated to include the latest rulings from the court and the authorizations of force.

However, there is the concept of qualified immunity for officers established by the Supreme Court. An officer will not be held liable for actions taken that may be in violation of federal constitutional rights if there was no clear law at the time. This grants officers some protection for actions taken during a use-of-force incident in areas where the issue may be gray. The case that established this was Bivens v. Six Unknown Named Agents for federal officials and 42 U.S.C. Section 1983 for state and local officers. This, of course, protects officers only from a suit and their actions may still be reviewed by the court. It shows that the courts do accept that the job of a law enforcement officer is one that has many sides to it and that all circumstances need to be considered. However, depending on the actions of a law enforcement officer and the circumstances, the court can remove this immunity, so officers need to be careful not to take action that is beyond the scope of their authority and guidelines.

Perhaps, one of the more well known of the Supreme Court rulings is Tennessee v. Garner. This case started out as police officers responding to a burglary call. On their arrival, they spotted Garner, as he was fleeing the scene. Officers pursued, and when Garner was about to climb a fence, one of the officers fired and killed Garner. The officers testified that they thought Garner would have escaped if he had climbed the fence and they estimated his age to be 17 or 18 years—he was, in fact, 15 years old. This case is often called the Fleeing Felon case. Before this, many police departments and even laws and the courts agreed that officers had the right to shoot fleeing felons. This ruling changed that, and now, officers do not have this ability, unless they can articulate that the person was a clear and present danger to others.

What was interesting in the Garner decision was that dissenting Justice O'Connor sided with the police, saying that they must make split-second decisions often in difficult conditions. However, the majority opinion written by Justice White said that the use of deadly force results in a seizure and that violated Garner's rights.

The case of Graham v. Connor sets up the concept of "objective reasonableness." Graham was a diabetic who had a friend drive him to a store to get some juice. The lines were long at the store, and so, Graham returned to his friend's car fairly quickly after entering the store. Officer Connor observed the behavior and believed that some type of crime may have occurred, and so, he stopped the vehicle. He detained the driver and Graham until other officers could arrive and checked the store to see if a crime had occurred. During this time, Graham was handcuffed, and he received some injuries. When no crime was found to have occurred at the store, Graham was released.

The court ruled that Officer Connor's actions were excessive force. The court then created several factors that the court would consider to see if the force applied by the police was appropriate and was termed objective reasonableness. The factors are as follows: (1) severity of the crime; (2) whether the suspect is an immediate threat to the public or the officer; (3) whether the person is actively resisting arrest or attempting to flee. Since this ruling, lower courts have also considered whether or not a warrant had been obtained before the incident.

An interesting case after which the Supreme Court decided that police officers can use less than lethal force against someone who poses a deadly force situation was Russo v. City of Cincinnati. The case involved a mentally impaired man who had barricaded himself in his apartment and was armed with knives. The confrontation between him and the police resulted in the taser being used multiple times, with little effect. The man was eventually shot by the officers as he came at them with the knives. There was a claim that the use of the taser in the incident was excessive force, and the court ruled that using less lethal means in a deadly force situation was permissible.

A case that cited Russo was Ewolski v. City of Brunswick. In Ewolski, the police utilized tear gas to try to get John Lekan to surrender after he had shot an officer. The police tried to gain entry into the residence where Lekan was hiding along with his wife and child. During the standoff, Lekan killed himself and his family members. The points that the court needed to consider here were the use of tear gas and an armored vehicle excessive force. The court ruled that using less lethal means in a deadly force situation, as in Russo, was not excessive force.

A similar case is Plakas v. Drinski. Plakas was suspected of driving under the influence (DUI) when he wrecked his car. He was spotted at a short distance from the accident and was brought back to the scene by one of the officers. During the follow-up at the scene, Plakas was arrested for DUI and placed in the back of the police vehicle that still had door handles in the rear seats. While driving to the police department, Plakas attempted to exit the vehicle, and when it was stopped, he was successful. He fled to a friend's house, where a confrontation took place, which ended up in a wooded area. He was armed at this point with a fireplace poker, which he obtained from the house. He was eventually shot and killed, as he charged one of the officers with the poker. The court ruled that the officers did not need to use less than lethal means to stop the aggression, as the officer did fear for his life.

With the cases of Plakas and Russo, we see that the court does look at the totality of the circumstances and apply the objective reasonableness standard to these cases. However, these cases emphasize why it is very important for you to articulate all that happens in the situation, so the court can have a clear view of what was occurring at the time. Writing a good, clear, and concise report is essential, as was mentioned in the chapter on report writing; write your reports like you want justices on the High Court to see.

However, in the case of Parker v. Gerrish, the court took a dim view of the use of the taser. Parker was being arrested for DUI, but he was being uncooperative because he would not cooperate during handcuffing. Parker held his hands so that Officer Gerrish could not apply the handcuffs and as a result used the taser on Parker to gain compliance. The court ruled that this was excessive force, as there was no direct threat to the officer that could lead him to use force other than that necessary to apply the handcuffs.

This is an example of the court looking at the circumstances and again taking into consideration what was taking place on the street. Yes, Parker was being uncooperative, but it was passive. The officer had other options that could have possibly been used, such as calling for backup to assist or utilizing an empty-hand technique to gain better control of Parker.

Similar to the Parker case, Bryan v. McPherson also had a ruling that the police used excessive force when a taser was deployed. Bryan was stopped for a traffic violation; however, he was upset and got out of the vehicle, ignoring the officer's commands to get back into the vehicle. As a result of his actions, the officer deployed the taser, and as a result, Bryan fell, which caused him injuries. Bryan was approximately 20 feet away from the officer when the taser was deployed, and as a result, the court said that he posed no immediate threat to the officer, as he was unarmed. This was also viewed by the court, as the taser is an intermediate use of force and must be deployed under those conditions, so basically, if you would use a baton, you could use a taser. This changed the way the taser was viewed on the use-of-force continuum and moved it above empty-hand techniques.

A case that shows that the court will look at the resistance or threat an officer faces when using force is Brown v. Cwynar. In this case, Cwynar was being disorderly, and the police were contacted. While there, they tried to detain Cwynar, but he attempted to get into his vehicle to flee the area. An officer was able to get Cwynar out of the vehicle and on the ground, but he would not cooperate when it came to being handcuffed. He was warned several times by officers that if he did not comply, he would be tased. An officer drive stunned him, while another applied the handcuffs. In the court's view, here, the amount of force used was proportional to the resistance, and so, this was not considered excessive force.

In a similar decision, the court found that a drive stun on a driver refusing to get into a police vehicle after being arrested was appropriate force in Gorman v. Warwick Township. Gorman had been stopped for a traffic violation, and subsequent investigation determined that she was DUI. She was arrested, and when the officer attempted to get her into the police vehicle, she stiffened her body and refused to cooperate. The officer applied the taser and was able to get her into the vehicle without further issues.

You will notice that many of these cases involve the deployment of the taser in these uses of force situations. This is partly because the taser was being evaluated by the court to see where it would allow the police to apply the tool and partly because this is a new form of force that the police can make use of. What is important for our discussion is how the court looks at the use of that force and under what circumstances.

This is why concepts like the use-of-force continuum, discussed in Chapter 1, play an important role when you apply force in a rapidly evolving situation. For example, in the case of Vinyard v. Wilson, the court ruled that the police used excessive force. In this case, Vinyard had been arrested for being disorderly. During the ride into the police department, Vinyard and the officer got into a heated exchange, in which the officer pulled the car to the side of the road and then utilized pepper spray on Vinyard. Keep in mind that Vinyard was under arrest, handcuffed, and in the backseat of the police vehicle. She posed no direct threat to the officer and was only arguing with him. You must be able to articulate the reason why you used that force and the threat you faced, so that the court can see why your actions were appropriate at that moment in time.

There are, of course, more cases that influence the use of force by the police. One thing you need to do is to seek out current cases yourself, so that you stay current on this issue, and to press your agency to do the same, as the court can shift its stance on an issue, as justices change positions and their influence is then felt in these decisions. It is important for training to also be updated and current.

When it comes to the issue of training, there is a rather well-known case that you should be familiar with; this case is City of Canton v. Harris. This is a landmark decision, much like Graham's and Garner's cases. This case says that an agency must adequately train officers in the tasks that they will be performing. The court used the term, "deliberate indifference," if an agency did not do this and violated section 1983 of the Federal Constitution. This means that each officer should receive adequate training in all areas in which they will be asked to perform, and if they are not trained, then the agency that they work for is liable.

As an officer, you are given responsibility and authority over others in society. An officer has the ability to take away someone's freedom and is authorized to use force to accomplish this. No other position in government has this authority than the law enforcement branch. As a result, there are restrictions placed upon when and where force can be applied, and it is extremely important that, when force is applied, law enforcement can articulate why and how it was applied. As long as the force use is applicable to the resistance being met, the court's decision will be in favor of the officer.

The following are some other cases that you may want to explore to see how the court ruled in the application of force by law enforcement.

United States v. Dotson, 49 F.3rd 227 (6th Cir 1995)

Montoute v. Carr, 114 F.3rd 181 (11th Cir 1997)

Deering v. Reich, 183 F.3rd 645 (7th Cir. 1999)

Porter v. City of Muncie, 2000 U.S. Dist LEXIS 7385 (S.D. Indiana, Indianapolis 2000)

Headwaters Forest v. Humboldt County 9817250 (9th Cir. 2000)

Cruz v. City of Laramie 239 F.3rd 1183 (10th Cir. 2001)

Deorle v. Rutherford, No. 9917188ap (9th Cir. 2001)

Martinez v. New Mexico Dept of Public Safety 47 Fed. Appx. 513 (10th Cir. 2002)

Isom v. Town of Warren Rhode Island, 360 F.3rd (1st Cir. 2004)

Kesinger v. Herrington, 381 F.3rd 1243 (11th Cir. 2004)

Scott v. Harris, 550 US 05–1631 (2007)

Crowell v. Kirkpatrick, 90–4100 (2nd Cir. 2010)

Glenn v. Washington County, 661 F.3rd 460 (9th Cir. 2011)

Nelson v. City of Davis, 10–16258 (9th Cir. 2012)

Aldaba v. Pickens, 13–7034 (10th Cir. 2015)

Final Thoughts

13

Amateurs talk hardware. Professionals talk software. It doesn't matter what's in your hand or between your legs. It matters what's in your heart and in your head.

—Lt. Col. Dave Grossman
The Bulletproof Mind, 2016

Lt. Col. David Grossman speaks about the three types of people in the world. There are the sheep. These are the people who go about their lives every day, work, play, and deal with issues that concern them and their family. Then, there are the wolves, who spend their time looking for opportunities to exploit the sheep or harm them. These are basically your criminal elements, terrorists or aggressors of any kind. Standing in their way are the sheepdogs. The sheepdogs watch over the sheep, protect them, direct them at times, and deal with the aggression of the wolves. Sheepdogs in life are people like the police and military. These are the people who are willing to risk their own life to protect the values of society and the sheep, who enjoy the benefits of that society.

When Col. Grossman talks about this, he mentions that, when looking at this, the sheepdogs perform a noble cause and serve the sheep. One thing to keep in mind, however, is that the sheep often resent the sheepdogs. They do not like the authority placed in sheepdogs or the ability of the sheepdogs to enforce rules on them. The sheepdogs are often not wanted until the wolves appear, and as soon as the danger has passed, the sheep once again have no desire to have the sheepdogs near. The sheepdogs perform their task even though appreciation does not come very often from the sheep; in fact, many times, the sheep resent the sheepdogs, but to keep the sheep safe, sheepdogs do their role anyway. It is a noble profession.

Throughout history, there have been sheepdogs. These are warriors; they are people who are willing to place their own life on the line to protect others' lives. Who else would run toward the sound of gunfire instead of going in the opposite direction? This defines the sheepdogs and is actually one of their strengths (Figure 13.1).

Developing the warrior mentality is vital to surviving a violent encounter. All through police training, there is emphasis placed on the community bond

Figure 13.1 John Niehaus, May 20,1928 to February 12,2011, 27 years of service.

and treating people with dignity and respect. This is, after all, what we expect from someone who represents society and law. The officer of the law is part of society, and there needs to be mutual respect from citizen and officer alike. This is separate from a violent confrontation. Here, the fight or flight instinct must take over, and for an officer, flight is not an option. If an officer flees, who then will stand there to protect the sheep?

The warrior mentality is one that digs deep when things seem bleak and is able to rise up to the challenge. Any first responder or sheepdog needs to have this in order to survive the incident. Mental toughness can be just as important as physical prowess. It is often the more determined person in a confrontation that actually wins the fight.

Along with the warrior mentality, the will to survive is also necessary. There may be a time when you find yourself in a fight and may be on the losing end. This is where the will to survive can aid you. In sports, we hear this all the time: never give up, keep going, or as the famous baseball player Yogi Berra said, "it ain't over 'til it's over." This means that as long as you have fight left in you, the fight goes on (Figure 13.2).

The survival instinct is strong in all of us. The ability to tap into that can aid us greatly in a time of great danger. The trick, of course, is not to let despair or panic overtake us. If we begin to panic in a violent encounter or begin to believe that we will lose, then it can become a self-fulfilling prophecy. You need the ability to dig deep within yourself and bring out all of your will power to survive.

Figure 13.2 Dondi Marsh, June 7,1956 to November 23,2006, 20 years of service.

There are examples of this all around us. One such example is the gunfight that took place between FBI agents and two bank robbery suspects around Dade County, Florida, in 1986. Michael Platt and William Matix had prior military training and were armed with automatic weapons; they were also on a robbery spree. The FBI were on a robbery stakeout, which drew them into direct conflict. Although there were seven FBI agents, the two armed robbers were willing to take them on.

The gun battle was not like something you would see on television or in movies but was real. Both sides were suffering injuries, and in the end, it came down to the two robbers still fighting and trying to get away, and one agent, though wounded, was trying to stop them. Agent Edmundo Mireles got up from his position of cover and walked toward the suspect vehicle, firing into the vehicle in a last ditch effort to stop them. His actions ended the fight. Had he not been able to draw upon his will to survive that encounter and his mindset of a warrior, the outcome might have been quite different.

Mental awareness and resolve are only the starter steps. The physical skills also need to be present. Traditionally, police training has presented training that is basically simple and a one-size-fits-all type. As any person who has been in an actual encounter will tell you, each situation is a rapidly evolving scenario and no one-size-fits-all program can cover it. We are all human and as such are susceptible to human concerns and conditions. The ability to have tools at our disposal in any kind of confrontation provides us the confidence that we will overcome the situation and for the sheepdog to be able to overcome that situation by using only the force necessary to succeed and be within department and legal guidelines.

There have been 10 fatal errors that have been identified by The Police Studies Council, which lead to officer fatality. These 10 errors are the following:

1. *Your attitude*: If you fail to keep your mind on the job while on patrol or you carry home problems into the field, you will start to make errors. It can cost you or other fellow officers lives.

2. *Tombstone courage*: No one doubts that you are police officers. However, in any situation, where time allows, wait for the backup. There are few instances where alone, unaided you should try to make a dangerous apprehension.

3. *Not enough rest*: To do your job, you must be alert. Being sleepy or asleep on the job is not only against regulations, but you endanger yourself, the community, and your fellow officers.

4. *Taking a bad position*: Never let anyone you are questioning or about to stop get in a better position than you and your vehicle. There is no such thing as a routine call or stop.

5. *Ignoring danger signs*: As a police officer, you will get to recognize "danger signs": movements, strange cars, and warnings that should alert you to watch your step and approach with caution. Know your beat and your community and watch for what is "out of place."

6. *Failure to watch the hands of a suspect*: Is he or she reaching for a weapon or getting ready to strike you? Where else can a potential killer strike but from their hands?

7. *Relaxing too soon*: The "rut" of false alarms that are accidentally set off. Walking in and asking if the place is being held up. Observe the activity. Never take any call as routine or just another false alarm. It's your life on the line.

8. *Improper use or no handcuffs*: Once you have made an arrest, handcuff the prisoner properly. Ensure that the hands that can kill you are safely cuffed.

9. *No search or poor search*: There are so many places to hide weapons that your failure to search is a crime against fellow officers. Many criminals carry several weapons and are able and prepared to use them against you.

10. *Dirty or inoperative weapon*: Is your weapon clan? Will it fire? How about the ammo? When did you last fire, so that you can hit a target in combat conditions? What's the sense of carrying any firearm that may not work?

By following these guidelines, officers will increase their officer safety. One of the things that have been reported by suspects who have killed police officers is that the officer is often described as being a nice person. Many times, officers will not follow proper procedure because they are trying to be nice, but in this line of work, you must be professional. General orders and police tactics are developed for a reason; following them will keep you and the community safe.

Presented here are concepts for you to build upon and mold to your own unique situation. These ideas come from centuries ago, during a time when you would not return home if you were not skilled. The Ninja of ancient Japan fought against a powerful and skilled opponent. They needed to use all of their abilities to survive any kind of confrontation, and the same is said of our present-day warriors.

Preparation for this encounter will enable you to not only draw upon those skills and training techniques but also use them in a way that allows you to perform at your best, no matter who your opponent is. Being in good physical shape, practicing defensive tactics techniques, and developing a mental resolve will all work in your favor.

However, keep in mind that once the combat of the moment has passed, the battle is not over. The report you write that explains your use of force can also be very important. Get the facts right, express yourself, and give details, so that someone who was not there will clearly understand what you faced and why you reacted as you did.

Being a sheepdog is not an easy path to follow. You are to be commended for selecting this path, but at the same time, understand that most sheepdogs walk this path without expectation of praise from the sheep. We will leave you with some thoughts to thank you for all that you do and to let you know that there are also those who understand the path that you have chosen.

Paul Harvey was a radio broadcaster from the 1950s to the 1990s. He presented his take on what it means to be a police officer. We would like to leave you with this thought from him.

> A Policeman is a composite of what all men are, mingling of a saint and sinner, dust and deity.
>
> What that really means is that they are exceptional, they are unusual, they are not commonplace. Buried under the froth is the fact: and the fact is, less than one-half of 1% of policemen misfit the uniform. And that is a better average than you would find among clergymen!
>
> What is a policeman? He, of all men, is at once the most needed and the most wanted. A strangely nameless creature who is "sir" to his face and "pig" or worse to his back (Figure 13.3).
>
> The policeman must be a minister, a social worker, a diplomat, a tough guy, and a gentleman.
>
> And of course, he'll have to be a genius … for he will have to feed a family on a policeman's salary."

Figure 13.3 Stan Morgan, September 14,1929 to January 1,2013, 25 years of service.

For more information or training opportunities, contact:

Stephen K. Hayes, Quest Center
6236 Far Hills Ave.
Dayton, Ohio 45459
937-436-9990
http://www.daytonquestcenter.com/

Bibliography

Barber, Sam. The Art of Empowerment. Presented at the *American Society for Law Enforcement Trainers*, Buffalo, NY, January 22–25, 1997.

Barnhart, Tracy. The Ultimate Use of Force Report retrieve from http://www.corrections.com/tracy_barnhart/?p=263, November 27, 2015.

Blauer, Tony. Spontaneous Protection Enabling Accelerated. Presented at the *American Society for Law Enforcement Trainers*, Richmond, VA, January 12–15, 2000.

Bruce, David. Predicting Assaultive Behavior. Presented at the *American Society for Law Enforcement Trainers Conference*, Richmond, VA, January 9–15, 2000.

Case Law 4 Cops, retrieved from http://caselaw4cops.net/use_of_force/use_of_force.htm January 9, 2016.

Christensen, Loren. Q & A with Tony Blauer. *The CrossFit Journal*, March 2012.

Cucci, Frank. SEALS Team Unarmed Combat Course Safe Technology, February 10, 2000.

Faulkner, Sam. Report Writing form Ohio Peace Officer Training Academy, 1998.

Faulkner, Sam. The Say What You Mean Drill form Ohio Peace Officer Training Academy, 1998.

Frazier, Joe; Dettloff, William. *Box Like the Pros*. HarperCollins, NY, 2005.

Grossman, Dave Lt. Col. *On Killing Little*. Brown & Co., 1995.

Grossman, Dave Lt. Col. Killology Research Group. Retrieved from http://www.killology.com/ November 27, 2015.

Hatsumi, Masaaki. Knife and Pistol Fighting, Yougen Corporation, Tsuchiya Bookshop, 1983.

Hayes, Stephen. *Ninja: Spirit of the Shadow Warrior*. Ohara Publications, 1980.

Hayes, Stephen. *Ninja Vol 2 Warrior Ways of Enlightenment*. Ohara Publications, 1981.

Hayes, Stephen. *Ninja Vol. 3 Warrior Path of Togakure*. Ohara Publications, 1983.

Hayes, Stephen. *Ninja Vol. 4 Legacy of the Night Warrior*. Ohara Publications, 1985.

Hayes, Stephen. *Ninja Vol. 5 Lore of the Shinobi Warrior*. Ohara Publications, 1989.

Hayes, Stephen. *Ninja Vol. 6 Secret Scrolls of the Warrior*. Sage Ohara Publications, 2007.

Hayes, Stephen. *Ninjutsu: The Art of the Invisible Warrior*. Contemporary Books, 1984.

Hayes, Stephen. *The Ninja Defense*. Tuttle Publications, 2012.

Los Angeles Police Department Training Bulletin Arrest and Control Los Angeles Police Department Vol. 28, Issue 12, June 1996.

McYoung, Marc. *Surviving a Street Knife Fight: Realistic Defensive Techniques*. Paladin Press, 1992.

Messina, Phil. Modern Warrior Ground Fighting Techniques Seminar Class in Kettering, Ohio, 1998.

Niehaus, Joe. Realistic Use of Force Training. *Law and Order Magazine*, June 1997.

Niehaus, Joe. Handgun Retention: Simpler is better. *The Police Marksman Magazine*, September/October 1998.

Niehaus, Joe. Warrior of the Mind. *Police Magazine*, July/August 1998.

Niehaus, Joe. Adding Realism to Your Handgun Retention Training. *The Police Marksman Magazine*, May/Jun 1999.

Niehaus, Joe. Going on Instinct: Behavior-Based DT Training. *The Police Marksman Magazine*, May/Jun 1999.

Niehaus, Joe. Knight Moves. *The Police Marksman Magazine*, November/December 1999.

Niehaus, Joe. The Chair: Use it to get a leg up on violent suspects. *Police Magazine*, January 2000.

Niehaus, Joe. Adding Spice to Realistic Training. *The Law Enforcement Trainer Magazine*, November/December 2002.

Outlaw Josey Wales Quotes; imdb retrieved from http://www.imdb.com/title/tt0075029/quotes November 29, 2015.

Police Poems retrieved from criminaljustice911.tripod.com/poems.html November 27, 2015.

Quotes about the Supreme Court. Retrieved from http://www.goodreads.com/quotes/tag/supreme-court January 8, 2016.

Rosenman, Samuel. *The public papers of Franklin D. Roosevelt, volume two: The year of crisis, 1933*. Random House, New York, 1938.

Ryan, Jack. Qualified Immunity in Use of Force Cases. PoliceLink Retrieved from http://policelink.monster.com/training/articles/2097-qualified-immunity-in-use-of-force-casesunited-states-supreme-court- January 9, 2016.

Seishinkan Sogobujutsu, Classical Sogo Warrior Martial Arts Sciences—Martial Arts Quotes retrieved from http://www.seishinkan.com/martial_resources/martial_ultimate_warrior_quotes_samurai_quotes.htm, November 28, 2015.

Siddle, Bruce; White, Wally PPCT Defensive Tactics Instructor Manual PPCT Management Systems 1989.

Smith, Martin, Tactics for Edge Weapon Confrontation presented at the American Society for Law Enforcement Trainers, Mobile Alabama 1998.

Supreme Court Quotes – BrainyQuote. Retrieved from http://www.brainyquote.com/quotes/keywords/supreme_court.html, January 8, 2016.

The Police Studies Council. The Ten Fatal Errors that have killed experienced law enforcement officers retrieved from http://www.theppsc.org/Archives/DF_Articles/Officers-Killed/Fed-Stats/1992_FBI_Study.htm, November 27, 2015.

Tueller, Dennis, Sergeant, Tueller Drill retrieved from https://en.wikipedia.org/wiki/Tueller_Drill, November 28, 2015.

Use of Force: Firearms and Related Issues. Retrieved from http://r.search.yahoo.com/_ylt=A0LEViTpBpFW9agAwx0nnIlQ;_ylu=X3oDMTByNXQ0NThjBGNvbG8DYmYxBHBvcwM1BHZ0aWQDBHNlYwNzcg--/RV=2/RE=1452373865/RO=10/RU=http%3a%2f%2fwww.pti.illinois.edu%2fresources%2fdocuments%2fUseofForce-FirearmsandRelatedIssues.doc/RK=0/RS=mdWCW6EVWJ42GNjfcXJvrk3IoXQ- January 9, 2016.

Use of Force Report Writing Guide obtained from http://www.aele.org/uof-rep-guide.pdf on November 27, 2015.

VanBrocklin, Valerie; Courtroom Testimony and Demeanor – How to be an effective witness 1994.

Index

Note: Page numbers followed by f refer to figures, respectively.